Leicester Haymarket Theatre
presents

Palace of Fear
by Philip Osment

theatre
Leicester Haymarket

Leicester
City Council

ARTS COUNCIL
ENGLAND

SDSA
School Development
Support Agency

Neighbourhood
Renewal Unit

More information from www.lhtheatre.co.uk

Palace of Fear

An epic fantasy journey written by Philip Osment

Cast

Aisha	Andrea Hall
Nicholae	Keith Saha
Mum	Natalia Campbell
Ada	Isabel Ford
Robert	David Fielder

Directed by	Adel Al-Salloum
Designed by	Nettie Scriven
Dramaturgy	Esther Richardson
Assistant Director	Dawn Bowden
Puppeteer	Sean Myatt
Lighting Designer	Mike Robertson
Composed by	Tom Bailey

Production Manager	Graham Lister
Stage Manager	Ruth Stanway
Wardrobe Supervisor	Lally Broome
Props maker	Elisa Bua Brownfoot

Developed in collaboration with the Year 5 children of Leicester schools: Crescent Junior, Eyres Monsell Primary, Northfield House Primary, St Barnabas Primary and Taylor Road Primary School.

Palace of Fear was originally commissioned by the Schools Development Support Agency of Leicester and was made possible through the generous support of the Neighbourhood Renewal Fund.

Thanks

Leicester Haymarket Theatre would like to thank all those involved in the development of this piece:

Peter Davies – St Barnabus Primary School
Dawn Gealy – Northfield House Primary
Norman Machin – Eyres Monsell Primary School
Howard McDermott – Crescent Junior School
Cherylin Norris – Taylor Road School
Robert Vincent – Leicester City LEA

The Company

Andrea Hall Aisha

Andrea gained acting experience by working with various youth and community projects throughout her teenage years, before working professionally. Her theatre credits include *Talkin' Loud* (Latchmere Theatre), *Breakin' News* (Oxfordshire Touring Theatre Company) *Hyacinth Blue* (Lyric Studio), *Johnny Dollar* (Bloomsbury Theatre), *Mind Your Head* (Fitures Theatre), *West Side Story* (Lost Theatre), *The Tempest* (Lost Theatre). Her Television credits include *TLC* for BBC Television.

Keith Saha Nicholae

Keith started acting at the Everyman Theatre, Liverpool. He then went on to train at Salford University and Hope St Project. Work includes *Making a Difference*, and *Make Some Noise* for Theatre Royal Stratford East, *Missing* and *Authentic Voices* for Theatre Centre, and Philip Osment's *Wiseguys* for Contact Theatre. He is also involved in writing new contemporary musical theatre and scores for Theatre Centre, Cardboard Citizens and Theatre Royal Plymouth. Directing includes *The Trouble with Richard* for Graeae Theatre Company. He is passionate about creating theatre and music with and for young people.

Natalia Campbell Mum

Natalia trained at Middlesex University and Lee Strasberg Studio. Some of her theatre credits include *Bollywood Jane* (Leicester Haymarket), *Taj* (The Big Picture Company), *Lalla's Big Day* (Kali Theatre Company), *Starfish* (Theatremongers), *Arabian Nights* & *Hunchback of Notre Dame* (OTTC) and *Bazaar* & *Rummage* (Edinburgh Festival). Television: *EastEnders, Casualty, Crimewatch* & Discovery Channel. Film: *Learn to Love*. Dance & Music: *Tango Argumentino* (South America Tour), *Mulan* for Walt Disney (Copenhagen) & *Sister India* (UK & Europe). Recently, Natalia was lucky enough to see her writing debut *Nothing but Dreams – The Musical* performed at the Greenwich Theatre.

Isabel Ford Ada

Isabel trained at Rose Bruford College of Speech and Drama. Her theatre credits include Leonna in Jean Anouilh's *The Orchestra* at Southwark Playhouse, Bertha in *Jane Eyre* and Fairy Bow Bells in *Dick Whittington* with Bob Carlton at The Queens' Theatre, Hornchurch. Missus in Debbie Isitt's production of *One Hundred and One Dalmations*, Mary Magdalen in *The Millennium Mysteries* with Teatro Biuro Podrozy, various roles in *Rumplestiltskin*, Mrs Twit in Roald Dahl's *The Twits* and Mary in *The Mysteries* with Macnas Theatre, all at The Belgrade Theatre, Coventry.

David Fielder Robert

David Fielder trained at the Central School of Speech and Drama, Birmingham in the early 70s. Since he has worked all over the country and the world with the National Theatre, Royal Shakespeare Company and Shared Experience, where he is a board member. He can be seen occasionally on TV as a 'baddie' usually in The Bill and permanently as an Olympic runner in *Superman III*.

Philip Osment Writer

Philip Osment read Modern Languages at Keble College, Oxford and then trained as an actor, appearing in several leading alternative theatre companies before turning to writing and directing. His plays include *Telling Tales*, *This Island's Mine* and *The Undertaking* for the Gay Sweatshop; *Who's Breaking?*, *Sleeping Dogs* and *Wise Guys* for Red Ladder, *Listen* for Theatre Centre, *The Dearly Beloved* and *What I Did in the Holidays* for the Cambridge Theatre Company, *Flesh and Blood* for Method and Madness and *Buried Alive* for the Hampstead Theatre/Theatre Royal, Plymouth. He received the Peggy Ramsay Award for *Little Violet and the Angel*.

Adel Al-Salloum Director

Adel has been the Associate Director at the Leicester Haymarket Theatre for two years and has worked alongside Philip in the development of this piece over the last eighteen months. Previously Adel directed Lynda Marshall Griffiths *Mine* for LHT which played in the studio before embarking on a tour of Leicester City Primary Schools. Before joining Leicester Haymarket Theatre Adel was the Associate Director for Northern Stage Ensemble where she directed *The Happy Prince* and *The Elves and the Shoemaker*. Since leaving Rose Bruford College Adel has worked extensively creating work with, and for, children and young people at: The Tricycle Theatre, Northern Stage Ensemble and Leicester Haymarket Theatre. Projects have ranged from creating sensory installations with Under 5s to healthy living film making projects with young people.

Nettie Scriven Designer

Since 1980 Nettie Scriven has designed for a variety of spaces, including schools, community centres, arts centres, studio theatres, art galleries and repertory houses. She represented the UK at the *Prague Quadrennial* in 1999. She is Senior Lecturer in Theatre Design at Nottingham Trent University. Productions include: *The Secret Garden*, Nottingham Playhouse; *A Little Princess*, Yvonne Arnaud; *Between Friends*, Komedia Theatre; *The Snow Spider* & *Aesop's Fables* Sherman; *Stepper Joe* and *The Waltz*, West Yorkshire Playhouse; *Crivelli's Garden*, Theatre Centre; *Rooms*, Glasshouses Dance Co; *One for Sorrow*, Hijinx; *Plague of Innocence* (1988 Best Young People's Production) & *The Lost Child,* Sheffield Crucible; *Hamlet*, Contact; and *The Scam*, Traverse. Most recently she designed and co-produced *Dragon Breath*, Made 2 Measure / Creative Partnerships/ NTU, and forthcoming productions include *One Dark Night* Sherman Theatre / Theatre Centre, *In Limbo* Classworks, *Journey to the River Sea* Unicorn / Theatre Centre.

Esther Richardson Dramaturgy

Esther is the director of Theatre Writing Partnership. As a Dramaturg she has worked on several productions for Leicester Haymarket Theatre including *Bollywood Jane* (by Amanda Whittington) and *The Illustrious Corpse* (by Tariq Ali). Before setting up Theatre Writing Partnership Esther was the Assistant Dramaturg for the RSC. She also works as a freelance theatre director.

Dawn Bowden Assistant Director

Dawn worked for 15 years as an actress, working in both theatre and television. Credits include *Godspell* (National Tour and Fortune Theatre London), *Groucho* (Comedy Theatre London), *Rock a Bye Sailor* (Theatre Royal Northampton) *The Merchant of Venice* (Phoenix Contemporary) *Magic Boat* (Polka Theatre), *Privates on Parade* (National Tour). She now works as a creative facilitator and director predominantly working with children and young people. Recent credits include *Macbeth*, and *Joseph and the Amazing Technicolor Dreamcoat*, both for Lutterworth Youth Theatre which she ran for 2 years, and *When a Bird Can't Sing* (Leicester Haymarket Theatre). Last year Dawn facilitated and directed *We Can Because We think We Can* – a large community event with 150 participants performed at the Leicester Haymarket Theatre. Most recently Dawn has been leading on and has been part of the creative team for a project that has brought 26 young people together from across the city of Leicester. The project culminated in a mixed media outdoor performance called *Captured Live* (Leicester Haymarket Theatre). She is delighted to have been part of the creative process for *Palace of Fear.*

Sean Myatt Object Animator

Sean was always interested in the art of puppetry, as a young boy and enjoyed bringing things to life whether a sock or a toy and has been lucky enough to do the same in his adult life, animating the inanimate. He trained at Nottingham Trent University as a Theatre Designer before embarking on professional life as puppeteer/Designer at Norwich Puppet Theatre. He was awarded the Arts councils training bursary to further develop his skills as puppeteer and performer where he met the Company Philippe Genty from France, this allowed him to work with Dancers, actors and animators in a truly unique form of visual theatre touring work to every continent of the world . In 1997 he founded Theatre Insomnia with Felicia Negomireanu, developing puppet theatre for both children and adults. More recently Sean has been asked to work as freelance puppet director to various Theatre companies in the UK.

Mike Robertson Lighting Design

A graduate of the Guildhall he works in most sectors of the lighting industry. In the theatre he has worked worldwide with hundreds of touring, West End and international credits. He has also worked extensively in television, concerts and live events. Outside of performance lighting he has created many architectural, aeronautic and commercial designs. Mike is a consultant to several national companies and has designed lighting for many roadshows, car launches, exhibitions and extensively for parties and outdoor events. His practice is www.lightingplan.co.uk.

Tom Bailey Composer

Tom Bailey has recently been concentrating on completing two new albums of his own work. Neon Heights long awaited second album — *A Hot Trip To Heaven* is released on November 1st 2004 and FUG have also completed a second album *Procrastinate* scheduled for release at the end of January 2005. Both albums are currently hotly tipped by the press. Tom has been fortunate enough to have been working as a songwriter, remixer and producer with some stunning talent. Projects in the last twelve months have included work with Alicia Keys, Sugababes, Grand National, Talib Kweli, Eric Sermon, Christina Aguilera & Alice Russell amongst others and is at present reworking tracks for Nina Simone's archive and a new mix for Jill Scott's current single *Golden*. Tom is still writing music for Film & Television. His company *Freakish Kid,* based in Budapest, Hungary is developing three animated series and two feature length films. Back home collaborations with film director Simon Ellis has seen them winning awards for their last two films at Festivals in Italy, Germany, Canada and the United States. It is a real pleasure for Tom to have been invited back once again to the Leicester Haymarket Theatre to contribute to this production — *Palace Of Fear*.

Philip Osment

PALACE OF FEAR

OBERON BOOKS
LONDON

First published in 2004 by Oberon Books Ltd.
(incorporating Absolute Classics)
521 Caledonian Road, London N7 9RH
Tel: 020 7607 3637 / Fax: 020 7607 3629
e-mail: oberon.books@btinternet.com
www.oberonbooks.com

A catalogue record for this book is available from the British Library.

ISBN: 1 84002 505 0

Contents

Introduction

IN JULY 2003 Adel Al-Salloum and I took an actress, a suitcase and some props into five schools in Leicester and began work with five classes just coming to the end of Year 4. Our aim was to find out what stories and characters the children were interested in. The actress played a woman who spoke no recognisable language and the children had to find out who she was. The session ended with them telling her how to get to an address in Leicester, which was written on a piece of paper she had in her suitcase. Each class arrived at a different reason for her being in their school, they had different ideas of her history and who the people were in the photos she carried.

This was my introduction to the children who inspired and informed the writing of *Palace of Fear.*

It was clear that although they enjoyed fantasy and magic they had to be encouraged to enter that world – when they did enter it their ideas where highly creative.

When Adel and I returned to work with these classes again in the autumn I decided to tell them a story, which took them into a magic forest of some sort. I began to tell them about Nicholae and Aisha whose mother was in some way lost to them.

The first storytelling session ended with them encountering a Guardian at the edge a forest. The children questioned this character and were obviously fascinated by this person and took turns to ask him questions. These questions appear in the script when Nicholae and Aisha meet the Guardian of the Forest.

We returned the following week with a specially commissioned sound tape and I told them about Aisha and Nicholae's experiences in the forest. When a creature that steals your mind came looking for them they had to lie still as in the party game Sleeping Lions and we played the tape and asked them what they could see and hear and smell. We tried to let them see that no answer was wrong and so we discovered that the children could smell dog poo or a bacon sandwich – neither of which seemed out of keeping with the story. One child said she could smell Mum just after she has got out of the bath. Some of them did drawings of what they saw which were particularly imaginative and vivid – a ghost, a vampire, a slimy thing with three heads. It was clear that a theme about fear was emerging.

For the next four weeks ten to fifteen children from each class joined children from the other schools in the Haymarket rehearsal room where we took the story further. Nicholae and Aisha followed the creature that could become the thing you fear most, into the ground. There they met a person standing in a boat who welcomed them with a smile and told them that she/he had been waiting for them. Our designer Nettie had provided large pieces of paper and paints and asked each child to lie down on their sheet of paper and make the shape of the figure who stood in the boat. Their partners traced their outline onto the paper and then each child painted this figure. They created the most extraordinary characters – some thought it was Mum, some that it was her best friend Trudy, for some it was Dad, for others it was a more mysterious ghostly figure.

In the next session I incorporated their discoveries from the previous week and took them into the Palace of Fear and in groups the children created a room with cloth and flats and other materials – each room had its special fear. In one room a boy crouched in a cardboard box – he was scared of being trapped; another room was full of spiders; another had sea creatures that would electrocute you; another room contained death itself. Once again the children showed great ingenuity and imagination and I was able to include their ideas in the next stage of the story.

For our third session in the rehearsal room I took the children to the point in the story where they met THE ONE WHO WEARS THE DEATHLY CROWN and their task was to enact the scene where the children eventually tricked him and discovered where Mum was hiding.

In my final storytelling session I took the children to the point where Nicholae and Aisha entered the Room of

Loneliness. While they went for a break we placed a bed in the middle of the space on which sat an actress they had never met. The children came back into the space and sat around the bed. In pairs, as Nicholae and Aisha, they tried to persuade Mum to come home with them. These scenes were heartfelt and moving. Eventually Mum went to deal with the One and I narrated the end of the story. Nicholae and Aisha returned to their home to find Mum waiting for them.

It was at this point I wrote the story down and it is included in this volume. I used it as a basis for the first draft of the play. With actors we presented this draft as a rehearsed reading to the same groups of pupils in March 2004. With their help we explored the text and listened to their responses.

After listening to their questions I felt I needed to understand the history or backstory of the characters and what I call the cosmology of the story. So I wrote the story of Grendel – also included in the volume.

The whole process was immensely nourishing for me as a writer. It was also very enjoyable – much more so than sitting at home in front of a screen trying to concoct a story. Many of the children's ideas fed directly into the play. The time I had spent with them also helped me to understand their concerns and relationships with each other and the adults involved which also influenced the script. It was a great privilege to work with the children and their teachers and I only hope they got as much out of the collaboration as I did.

Philip Osment
August 2004

FAMILY TREE

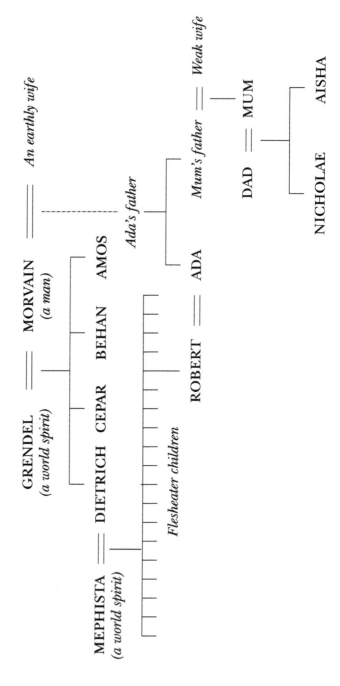

The Death of Grendel
The Myth behind *Palace of Fear*

AND IN THE TIMES before the great Creation when all was dark and the cosmos was a lifeless, cold and empty place there was just the longing for life. And the longing came upon the dark and created light and it came upon the cold and created heat and it came upon the empty and created matter. And the spirits were born who were to rule each Universe and planet. They were to be the guardians of life in their Universe and their Mother's womb was the dark and the cold and the empty and their father's seed was the light the heat and the matter. And the spirits crept out into the endless night and waited for time to begin.

And each was allotted a time and place that was fitting.

But out in the dark and the cold and the empty there was another longing: this was the longing for death. It was a longing for nothingness and it was a powerful force but it was nowhere to be seen.

And when Universes were formed the spirits descended onto worlds where life might flourish and took form. And on a blue and green planet where water was in plenty and where the sun shone, the spirit of the Earth descended to create the creatures that came out of the sea and the mud and the forests and the swamps. And her name was Grendel and she watched over the creatures and loved them all. For were they not all the offspring of the fertile earth?

And in those days Man was just one of the creatures that roamed the earth – both predator and prey, hunting weaker animals for his food and sometimes becoming the food of animals stronger than him. It was a dangerous and precarious existence.

And like all creatures, Man tried to protect his offspring. He lived in caves with others of his species and hunted in packs and kept fires burning at night to scare away the wild beasts that lurked in the darkness. But sometimes the fire would die out and he would wake to find that something had come from the swamp or the forest or from the shadows at the back of the cave to steal away the baby sleeping at his side.

So he learnt to fear. Fear was his protection from the unknown. When he was threatened, fear sent messages from his brain to his limbs and released chemicals into his bloodstream so that he could run faster and fight harder.

And Grendel watched from her sacred lair at the heart of the forest and in time she began to love Man more than her other creatures. She loved him for his cleverness and resourcefulness and for his imagination. She would see him sit at night around the fire outside his cave, with his wife and children, with his brothers and sisters; his parents, his aunts and uncles; sometimes even with his grandparents (although few of his kind lived to be a grandparent). She watched them eating and talking and planning and singing and dancing. And she listened to their stories. Most of all she loved them for these stories they told each other as the flames threw their shadows against the rocks. And she crept closer because she wanted to hear the stories so much. She needed to know what became of the brave hunter on the plains as he stalked his prey for miles and what happened when he died and returned to the stars where his light still burns in the night sky. She smiled at the way man imagined what his life would be like after death. What a piece of work was this creature! How she loved him.

This was Grendel's downfall. For was it not ordained that no spirit should become so attached to one of her creatures that she loved it more than the rest?

One storyteller there was whose voice was sweeter than the honey in the bees' nest, whose hair flowed over his shoulders like the cascading waters of the river, whose eyes were deep pools of emerald, whose lips were ripe fruit that made Grendel's mouth water. His name was Morvain and when he told stories the whole clan listened wide-eyed and breathless. With his words he painted pictures in their minds that terrified them and made them laugh and weep and dream. Listening to him Grendel also wept and laughed and dreamt.

Night after night she crept closer to the camp knowing she was in danger of revealing her secret existence. For no creature was allowed to look on the Spirit of the World and live to tell the tale. If one came within range of her or set eyes on her, she devoured it. For so it was ordained.

But the stories of Morvain worked on her like a drug so that she exposed herself as she crept out of the forest and even the flickering lights of the fires could not keep her away.

Night after night she returned. And sometimes the fire died and she would do what no World Spirit should ever do. She crept into the cave to where Morvain slept and crouched and stared at his beautiful face until the dawn drew a line of light on the horizon and she had to tear herself away.

Then one day the rains came and the river turned to a raging torrent and flooded the plains and rose until all the land was covered in water.

When the storms abated and the water receded Grendel approached the cave but Morvain had disappeared with the rest of his clan. And Grendel wept at the loss and her howls could be heard in the night and sent all creatures that had survived the flood hurrying home to their lairs.

For many days and nights she searched for traces of the humans.

Then one night as she climbed over a mountain range she smelt smoke drifting up from the valley below. As she descended she found a ledge where bones of a mountain deer were scattered. Looking down she saw the fires of a human settlement. She climbed lower till she reached a rock just above their camp. She recognised the humans. They were Morvain's clan but

Morvain was not there. Again she wept because she thought that he had drowned in the waters of the flood.

The moon came out from behind a cloud and she turned away to return to the forest:

There he stood in her path – his eyes wide, but not in terror. In wonder. He somehow knew that he was not looking on any earthly creature.

And Grendel too stared. The moon shone on his mane of hair and turned it silver. His eyes shone.

'Go, Man,' she told him, 'Go, you must not look on me!' And her voice was the voice of the Heavens. It would terrify most mortals and make them turn and run.

But as she spoke Morvain's lips curled into a smile.

'Oh creature of the night,' he said to her, 'Don't send me away now that I have found you. You who have come to me so often in my dreams. Let me but stay with you a little while.'

'You must go,' she told him, 'If you don't, I must kill you!' But still he didn't move.

'How could something so beautiful ever be so cruel?' he asked her. And instead of leaving he came closer and he touched her cheek with his hand. And as he did, Grendel shivered, for no creature of her earth had ever been allowed to come so close, let alone touch her. It was not permitted.

'You would not kill me, would you?' he asked.

And Grendel felt herself drown in his eyes that she now saw were flecked with gold.

'I must,' she said and never had her powerful voice of the rivers and the mountains and the wide plains and the vast oceans trembled so.

'Then kill me!' he said as he pulled the furs covering him apart and bared his chest and soft throat to her.

She could see a vein pulsing in his neck and in that moment she knew she could not kill him.

'Tell me a story,' she said, 'And then I might not kill you.'

And so that night and for many nights after, he told her stories of the trees and plants and creatures and rocks and stories of the stars above.

This was how Grendel was tamed. She came to love Morvain as a woman loves a man and showed him all the secrets of the earth – the places where the animals came at night to drink, how to get nutrition from their milk and from the eggs of the birds; she showed the spots in the forest where the plants grew that could be used for medicines, the most fertile places where crops could be grown and where the fruit hung heavy on the trees. She showed him the hard gemstones and precious ores that lay concealed in the rocks and the earth. Little did she know what Morvain would do with the knowledge!

And their love increased with the days and Morvain the storyteller became the husband of the Spirit of the Earth and together they had four sons. The first child they called Dietrich, the second, Cepar, the third Behan and the youngest was Amos. Amos was Morvain's favourite and he had his father's eyes and golden hair.

Grendel and Morvain were only together at night. Their days were spent apart. Grendel longed for the night and paid little attention to what was happening to the other creatures under her protection. She did not see how Man was beginning to hunt and kill them in ever greater numbers using new weapons made not from stone but from iron. Morvain had used the materials that Grendel had shown him to fashion new and deadlier weapons, which gave man an advantage over his prey. And his numbers increased and he began to dominate the other species. He began to breed the animals for their meat and their milk and their hides. He built dwellings and villages that he fortified to protect himself against the wild beasts and against other clans. Not only did he hunt and kill animals – sometimes he hunted and killed his own kind.

The animals retreated deeper into the forest and came to Grendel to complain but, blinded by her love, she did not listen to their complaints. Only Dietrich listened and he grew angry with his mother for continuing to favour men. From the mountain Dietrich had spied on his father and watched him going about his daily business. He had seen him being elected king of his people because of all the things he had done for them with the knowledge he had gained from Grendel. Dietrich had watched as the men of the tribe displayed their daughters in front of Morvain and urged him to take one of them as his wife. He had watched as Morvain began to sit with one girl in particular – a girl who had shown least interest in his attention because she thought him too grand to look on her. And later he watched the marriage celebrations. Now he saw the golden haired children that played around Morvain's feet when he told stories in the evening.

But still, in the dark of night, Morvain would creep from his hut to be with Grendel. In the village they said he practiced magic and that he spoke to demons in the night but while he brought them wealth and prosperity they turned a blind eye to his nocturnal wanderings.

Dietrich was filled with anger.

'He has a woman from his own people,' he told his mother, 'He doesn't care about us!'

But Grendel would sigh and defend Morvain. 'He had to take a wife. His people expected that of him, but it is us that he loves,' she told her son.

Man started to come deeper and deeper into the forest. There were less creatures now to complain to Grendel but she was forced to see that things were getting out of control. If Man reached the heart of the forest his presence would defile the sacred home of Grendel herself – the hidden lair where she had lived for centuries which she now shared with her four sons.

Dietrich raged at his mother for her blindness and his brothers tried to calm him. Dietrich wanted to fight man and destroy his homes but Grendel forbade it.

'We are here to protect all creatures,' she told him.

'So why aren't you protecting all the creatures that man is killing?' he replied. 'He has killed so many that soon there will be none of them left!'

Then Behan the second brother would say, 'Stop quarrelling, I'm trying to get some sleep!'

'You're meant to be guarding our home and all you do is sleep,' grumbled Dietrich.

Cepar would try to pacify his older brother by taking him out to sea in his boat to watch the sea creatures.

'Man can't reach us here,' he said to reassure him, 'He doesn't come out here.'

'Yet!' was Dietrich's short reply.

It was only Amos who could calm his brother. He did it by telling stories. He had inherited his father's love of weaving words into pictures that evoked tears and laughter. He told of the eternal fight between the longing for life and the longing for death. How Universes were created by the longing for life filling the void with matter that exploded out. This was how the stars and the planets were formed. And he told how the longing for death watched and waited for the stars to die and for the Universes to contract again until each one was just a tight tiny mass. And the longing for death made a crown of jewels made of collapsed Universes that could not be seen even though they contained the matter of many worlds and many stars. Each jewel was so heavy that everything was pulled back into its centre and not even light could escape from it. This was why not a single jewel could be seen. And the crown was called the Deathly Crown and awaited the One who would come to wear it and who would destroy all matter so that the endless circle of life and death would cease and nothingness would be eternal.

He told stories of the birth of the Spirits in the time before Creation. How their Mother came out of the empty cold night down into the warm daylight world. He told them of the other spirits who dwelt in other Universes. Universes that existed beyond rifts in space and time.

'Tell us about Mephista,' his brothers would say to him.

And Amos would tell them the story of Mephista. Mephista was a beautiful spirit who had been allotted one of the loveliest worlds in any Universe. But Mephista was fearful of what would happen when she descended to her world. She liked too much to float in the ether out beyond the stars. She didn't want to become matter and live a life that was limited by weight and size and density. And she went out to the farthest reaches of the cosmos and felt the pull of the Deathly Crown. She could sense its presence even though she could not see its light. 'If I had that I would be able to rule all known Universes,' she told herself. And she reached out and grabbed the crown just as her allotted Universe came into being. And Mephista tumbled down, down, down onto her lovely world but the crown fell into one of its deepest oceans. Because it was so heavy it penetrated deep into the depths and though she looked for it for many aeons she could not find it.

Meanwhile, on her lovely world, life came into being. It was soon teeming with creatures of all kinds. But Mephista took no joy in the life around her. She grieved for the loss of the Deathly Crown. She grew to hate the living beings of her world. Just by touching the crown she had become wicked and cruel and had no desire to nurture life. The creatures were toys to be played with and discarded. Mephista took joy in taking the form of their greatest fear and watching them as they stood before her paralysed with terror. Then she would transform herself into a stream of snakelike matter that would enter her victims and steal away their wills. The helpless creatures would be unable to flee and she would slowly devour their flesh – often keeping them alive for days. Soon her world was a barren wasteland where nothing grew or flourished and sandstorms blew across its face so that Mephista retreated to the underground depths where she looked in vain for the Deathly Crown. She had broken the eternal laws of creation. Instead of encouraging life she had destroyed it, instead of fullness she had created emptiness, instead of fertility she had created barrenness. It was ordained that she should never be allowed to leave that place. She was no longer a guardian spirit for she had no Universe to guard.

His brothers listened to Amos entranced and Grendel would smile at the way he had taken what she had taught him about the spirit world and woven it into a rich tapestry of legends and myths.

As Dietrich listened the frown would slowly disappear from his brow.

'Perhaps one day Mephista will find the crown and then she will have power over us all,' he said.

'Oh yes, she wants that,' Grendel told him, 'The Crown would allow her to make rifts in her Universe so that she could cross over to new worlds where there are lives, and wills for her to control, and flesh for her to devour. But she is weak because there is no life on her world to sustain her and without the crown she does not have the power to create the rifts. Besides we the spirits of the other Universes won't allow it. If she ever tried to cross over she knows that we would be waiting for her.'

'But what if you weren't here?' her eldest asked.

His brothers looked at him in horror. He was saying the unthinkable.

'What do you mean?' his mother asked him.

'What if Man destroyed you and you weren't here to protect this world?' Dietrich persisted wanting to hurt her and punish her for her love for their father.

'No earthly creature can destroy one of us,' his mother replied, 'we are too strong for them!'

'But Man has gained powers that he should never have gained because you gave them to him!'

'Enough, Dietrich!' Her voice was full of anger and the earth quaked to hear it.

But Dietrich would not stop and storms ravished the world as they quarrelled until Dietrich took himself off to the tall mountains, where, above the clouds, he raged against his mother's folly.

Meanwhile Man was cutting down trees for timber. With it he made bigger dwellings and built fences to keep in his livestock. Timber helped him to be strong and to keep fear at bay. And Mothers told their children that there was no need to be afraid – no wild beast could come out of the dark to take them off to its lair. 'See how high are our fences,' they said, 'See how thick are our walls! What wild beast could ever jump that high or claw it's way through that.'

Man started to make boats to go out over the waters to fish and to explore and Cepar was sad to see that Dietrich had been right and that even the giant animals of the deep were not safe from Man. And all the time the forest diminished.

Morvain himself was alarmed to see what was happening and he tried to persuade his people to stop cutting down the trees and leave enough animals so that there would be pairs to breed in future years. But they grumbled at him and accused him of becoming weak. The priests of their new religions said that the king was still in the grip of the old superstitions and that he didn't believe in the all-powerful male God in whom they believed. Did he not nightly consort with demons from the forests?

From his mountain top Dietrich saw that his Mother's home would soon be discovered and so he started to fight back. If she wouldn't do anything about the menace then he would. He made raids in the night on the settlements of man. He would swoop down from the mountain and destroy the wooden homes, slashing and killing as he went. In the mornings there was the sound of weeping and wailing as the humans counted their losses and buried their dead. They built higher and thicker fences but Dietrich could sweep them aside with a single blow as if they were made of reeds.

Once again fear stalked the humans. They were not used to feeling it and they were angry and in a state of panic. They came to Morvain and demanded that he do something.

'This has been done to us by the demons of the forest,' they shouted, 'We must root them out and destroy them before they destroy us!'

When Morvain tried to reason with them and to explain that they had brought this destruction on themselves by their greed, they jeered at him.

'Perhaps you want us to go back to living in caves!' one shouted.

'Go and live in the forest with the beasts if that's how you feel,' said another.

And in their forges they melted the metal to make more weapons.

And still Dietrich attacked. He grew to love the smell of their fear. It was sweeter to him than the sweetest-smelling perfume. He hungered for it when he was away from it. Sometimes in the middle of one of his nocturnal raids he stood amidst all the blood and destruction and inhaled in ecstasy. So much fear around him – fear that he had created. Now his Mother would see just what he could do. Now his father would know who was weak and who was strong.

Morvain could no longer visit Grendel every night. The people watched him and he feared he might lead them to her. He was growing older now and the people chose a new king – a king who believed in the new God and who was a warrior not a storyteller. This new king drove his people on to prepare for war.

'We will burn down the forest,' he told them, 'We will drive every demon from this earth till there is one God alone.'

And Morvain looked on sadly and feared for Grendel and his sons. He feared too for the children of his human wife. His son, Kamur, was confused. He was always quick to protect his father but it was now very dangerous to say anything against the new religion or against the preparations for war. And maybe his father was wrong and the new king was right. Maybe they had to lay claim to the world and reign over it as the supreme beings worshiping only one God.

And soon the new king had built a mighty army and in the forges the smiths had made axes and saws with giant teeth. They advanced on the forest and lit torches to scare the demons and to burn the wood once they had felled the trees. And Grendel saw too late that Man had become too strong.

Behan stood watched from the tall trees as man came closer to their sacred glade and Cepar urged his Mother to escape in his boat and trust their fate to the oceans.

'I cannot leave the sacred home in the forest,' she told him.

'Why not, Mother?' Amos asked her.

'Because it is the portal to beyond,' she said and I cannot leave it unguarded.

'Is it a rift in our Universe?' he asked incredulously.

'Yes, my sons,' Grendel told them. 'The world spirit communes with the cosmos from where it came by means of the portal in its dwelling place. For me the portal is the pool in our glade. Through it I talk with the spirits from other worlds and from other Universes. We cannot let Man find it because he is not ready to cross over.'

'But he's getting closer,' said Behan, 'Look over there, that is not the dawn. That is the light of the fires that burn where he has chopped and sawn down the forest.'

'I must stay,' said Grendel quietly. 'When the time comes, you and Cepar and Amos must pass through.'

'I would never leave you mother,' said Amos.

She smiled at him and stroked his hair and her hand was like the breeze fanning the tops of the trees which brought the smell of burning to their noses.

They watched helplessly as the trees fell and the fires came closer. And Dietrich descended from the mountain and called to his brothers to come out and fight the Men as he went amongst them slashing and killing. But their numbers were now so great. Their machines threw huge boulders into the air which crashed down and made the earth shake so that even Dietrich was forced to take shelter. And he ran to the sacred glade and found his mother and brothers.

'This is what you have done, Mother, he called to her. You have brought this on us!'

'My sons,' she said, 'You must go through before it is too late. You must call out to the spirits of the other Universe and they will give you entrance to their worlds.'

'You must come with us, Mother,' Amos cried.

'No I must stay here and close the portal once you have passed through,' she said.

'Then we're not leaving,' Amos told her.

And men broke through the trees holding burning torches and spears. Man stood in the sacred glade and Grendel wept in anguish.

'Go,' she told them, 'Before it is too late!'

And men were burning the sacred glade and arrows rained out of the night on Grendel and her sons.

'Go,' Grendel roared as she spread herself over her sons to protect them so that the deadly poison from the arrows entered her body alone – poison from the plants that she herself had shown Morvain all those years ago.

And she pushed her sons towards the pool in the burning glade as men on horses brandishing sharp swords bore down on them.

Dietrich saw that they had no choice and he it was that gathered his brothers and urged them to jump into the pool.

'Invoke the spirits,' their mother called to them.

So they sprang towards the pool and as he hovered in the air, with spears and arrows falling in the water around him, Dietrich called to his mother:

'I will be back. I will take revenge for this.'

'No!' Grendel pleaded, 'That is not the way!'

Her sons descended towards the pool. Just before Dietrich's head went beneath the water Grendel heard the name she least wanted to hear as he invoked the spirit he had chosen to give them refuge.

'Mephista!' he cried.

And their bodies disappeared into the pool leaving the surface rippling in the light of the fires.

The rain falls on the smouldering remains of the forest and the smoke rising from the blackened earth drifts across the swamp towards a rocky outcrop.

Two men clamber slowly over the stones pausing to drink from a pool that has gathered in a natural basin in the rocks. The young one has blond hair and emerald eyes with flecks of gold. The older one – his father maybe – has hair that is turning grey. He looks like a broken man – a man whose dreams have ended in disappointment and have proved no more substantial than the wisps of smoke that curl above the tree stumps.

They head towards some caves that can be seen in the rock face. The rain comes down in sheets and the water drips from their noses and beards and off their coats made of animal hide. They pause at the entrance to each cave to peer into the gloom and then move to the next one.

Are they looking for shelter or are they searching for something in particular?

Suddenly the younger man shouts. The older rushes towards him and for a moment they both stare into the cave. They confer for a while and then the older man enters the cave and the younger sits cross-legged in the rain.

Inside the cave Grendel is dying. Her life's blood has been poisoned and her wounds are many. The spirit of the world faces her end in a dark gloomy cave. As Morvain approaches she looks up and whimpers and as he looks on her he feels a pain in his chest that makes him gasp and the tears mix with the rain dripping from his cheeks.

'I knew you would find me,' she says in a low voice.

He goes to embrace her but she waves him off. 'We have no time for that,' she tells him, 'I have so much to teach you and so little time. The future of this world now depends on you, my love – on you and on your descendants. You must defend the world from the evil that the longing for death has unleashed in the cosmos. I fear that our son, Dietrich, will one day return with the power to destroy. He will try to take revenge on you and your kind.'

'Perhaps we deserve it,' said Morvain, 'Look at what we have done to this world! I tried so hard to stop it but it was too late. If only I could take back all the knowledge that I gave my people.'

'You cannot go back,' Grendel told him, 'Only forward. The knowledge I gave you has made your people strong – stronger even than the Earth Spirit herself. Now I am dying and your people must become the guardians of this world. You must learn how to value every creature on it and every plant and see how the lives of all are connected to each other. And where this is forgotten and where greed and fear cause man to destroy the life around him, there will the rifts appear that will allow the One Who Wears the Deathly Crown to enter your world. So now, I am giving you, and you alone, more knowledge, the knowledge of how to recognise the peculiar whirlpools of energy that occur when a rift is forming; the knowledge of how to combat the influence of the longing for death; the knowledge of how to fight the work of the One Who Wears The Deathly Crown. Your children and your children's children must be the ones who resist and save your people from the destruction that would come with his victory. He must never succeed. If he gains power over this world then he will easily conquer the whole cosmos.'

Outside the rain has stopped falling and the sun comes out and makes the steam rise from the young man's coat. He feels the warmth of it on his back. Kamur, for it is he, peers into the cave and wonders how long they are going to be talking. From time to time he hears his father's voice, asking a question or seeking verification but it is mainly Grendel's urgent whisper that he hears, a whisper which grows weaker all the while.

And the sun dips into the smoky haze on the horizon in colours that Kamur has never seen before and still his father and Grendel talk.

He lights a fire as the night grows colder.

As the moon rises he hears a sound that comes from somewhere deep in the cave like a great sigh and the sigh passes over Kamur and over the rocks and the tree stumps and the scorched earth, over the returning armies and the cities of man, over the oceans where boats now bob on the water, over the mountains and up into the skies.

And as Kamur looks up a star shoots across the firmament.

He feels Morvain's hand on his shoulder and looking up he sees tears in his father's eyes.

'She is gone,' he says.

And later as they sit after their meal staring into the flames Morvain tells his son a story:

'And in the times before the great Creation when all was dark and the cosmos was a lifeless, cold and empty place there was just the longing for life. And the longing came upon the dark and created light and it came upon the cold and created heat and it came upon the empty and created matter. And the spirits were born who were to rule each Universe and planet. They were to be the guardians of life in their Universe and their Mother's womb was the dark and the cold and the empty and their father's seed was the light the heat and the matter. And the spirits crept out into the endless night and waited for time to begin.'

Characters

AISHA
seven years old

NICHOLAE
her brother, ten years old

MUM
their mother

ADA
a woman from beyond the rift

ROBERT
her husband

THEODORE
a silver animal (a puppet?)

THREE GUARDIANS
all look identical Behan, Cepar and Amos

MEPHISTA
a snaky presence

THE ONE
a roar

HENRY THE CLAUSTROPHOBE
a person without a will

ARACHNOPHOBE
a person without a will

RAT

*The play could be performed by five actors possibly
using masks and puppets.*

Palace of Fear was first performed on 20 September 2004 at Eyres Monsell Primary School, Leicester, with the following cast:

AISHA, Andrea Hall

NICHOLAE, Keith Saha

MUM, Natalia Campbell

ADA, Isabel Ford

ROBERT, David Fielder

Director, Adel Al-Salloum

Designer, Nettie Scriven

Dramaturgy, Esther Richardson

Assistant Director, Dawn Bowden

Object Animator, Sean Myatt

Lighting, Mike Robertson

Composer, Tom Bailey

Production Manager, Graham Lister

Stage Manager, Ruth Stanway

Wardrobe Supervisor, Lally Broome

Props maker, Elisa Bua Brownfoot

Developed in collaboration with the Year 5 children of
Crescent Junior, Eyres Monsell Primary,
Northfield House Primary, St Barnabus Primary
and Taylor Road Primary School.

Scene 1

AISHA is eating a bowl of cereal. NICHOLAE enters with a bowl.

NICHOLAE: She didn't want any breakfast.

AISHA: Isn't she getting up?

NICHOLAE: No.

AISHA: Is she going to stay in bed all day?

NICHOLAE: I don't know.

AISHA: What's she doing?

NICHOLAE: Writing in her book.

AISHA: Again?

NICHOLAE: Yes.

AISHA: What do you think she's writing?

NICHOLAE: We're going to be late for school.

AISHA: I'm ready.

NICHOLAE: You haven't got your jumper.

AISHA: I don't want to wear it.

NICHOLAE: You've got to.

AISHA: It's dirty.

NICHOLAE: You can't go to school without a jumper on.

AISHA: Yes I can.

NICHOLAE: No you can't.

AISHA: I don't have to do what you say.

NICHOLAE: Yes you do.

AISHA: No I don't.

NICHOLAE: I'm older than you. You're only seven.

AISHA: I'm nearly eight.

NICHOLAE: Yeah well, I'm ten.

AISHA: So?

NICHOLAE: So you have to do what I say.

AISHA: No, I don't.

He taps her.

Aowwhh.

NICHOLAE: You've got to wear your jumper.

AISHA: You hit me.

NICHOLAE: Mum never lets you go to school without your jumper.

AISHA: She's not here. She doesn't care.

NICHOLAE: Yes she does.

AISHA: So why doesn't she get up and make our breakfast? She always makes our breakfast. There wasn't even any milk this morning. I had to have water on my sugar pops.

She cries more.

NICHOLAE: I'll buy some milk tonight.

AISHA: I'm not wearing my jumper.

NICHOLAE: Why not?

AISHA: Because it's dirty and no-one will sit beside me at school.

NICHOLAE: What you mean?

AISHA: They say I smell.

NICHOLAE: I told you to have a bath.

AISHA cries more.

I'll wash your jumper tonight.

AISHA: I want things to go back how they were before. Before Daddy went away.

NICHOLAE: Finish your breakfast.

AISHA: Is he never coming back?

NICHOLAE: Of course he is.

AISHA: Mum says he's gone for good.

NICHOLAE: No, he hasn't.

AISHA: Sally Mitchell's daddy went away and never came back.

NICHOLAE: You haven't told anybody, have you?

AISHA: What?

NICHOLAE: About Dad leaving. About Mum staying in bed all day writing in her book?

AISHA: No.

NICHOLAE: Aisha!

AISHA: I just told Kiera that you had to do all the washing and ironing.

NICHOLAE: I told you not to. You can never keep a secret.

AISHA: Can't I even tell Miss MacKendrick?

NICHOLAE: No! They'll come from the council and put us in a children's home and we won't be able to look after Mum.

AISHA: She should be looking after us.

NICHOLAE: Shut up!

AISHA: Shut up yourself. You were crying in your sleep last night.

NICHOLAE: No, I wasn't.

AISHA: You were having a nightmare.

NICHOLAE: I wasn't.

AISHA: Were.

NICHOLAE: Are you ready?

AISHA: Nearly.

He picks up the keys.

NICHOLAE: She says we have to lock all the doors and windows and make sure the curtains are drawn.

AISHA: Why?

NICHOLAE: She says you never know who's out there.

He stops by the fridge and feels into space.

AISHA: Is it the council?

NICHOLAE feels into space by the fridge.

Nicholae?

NICHOLAE: It makes me shiver here.

AISHA: You're by the fridge.

NICHOLAE: Mmmm.

AISHA: Is it the council out there?

NICHOLAE: What? Yeah. I don't know.

AISHA: I don't want to go to school.

NICHOLAE: We have to.

AISHA: Why?

NICHOLAE: Because if we don't they come round here and then they'll find out about Mum. Come on.

AISHA: Well, I'm not wearing my jumper.

NICHOLAE: Okay. Come on!

Scene 2

Sound of school bell, children in playground, teachers etc. It is 3:30. AISHA and NICHOLAE have just returned from school.

AISHA: I don't want noodles.

NICHOLAE: Too bad.

AISHA: I want Mum's Tarka Dal and rice.

NICHOLAE gets out three pot noodles.

AISHA goes to get the kettle.

NICHOLAE stands by the fridge and puts his hand out as if he thinks there's something there.

AISHA returns.

What are you doing?

NICHOLAE: I'll do that.

AISHA: I can do it.

NICHOLAE: No you can't. You're too young.

AISHA: No, I'm not.

They struggle over the kettle.

NICHOLAE: Mum doesn't let you.

ADA enters.

ADA: Ah, there you are. You're back.

They stare at her in amazement.

Robert! They're here. Now you must be Nicholae.

NICHOLAE: Uh –

ADA: And you're Aisha.

They stare at her.

AISHA: Are you from the council?

ADA: What? From the council? No! I'm Aunty Ada. I've come to look after you for a while.

AISHA: We haven't got an Aunty Ada.

ADA: Well, I'm not your Aunty Ada, I'm your Mother's Aunty Ada. That makes me your great aunt, doesn't it?

NICHOLAE: How did you get in?

ADA: I beg your pardon?

NICHOLAE: All the doors were locked.

ADA: Robert! They're back.

ROBERT enters.

This is Uncle Robert.

ROBERT: Hello kids.

AISHA: Where's Mum?

ADA: Your Mummy's fine, darling. She just needs a little rest. Now, I've made some dinner. I hope you like steak.

She brings two plates.

Sit down.

ROBERT: Mmmmmmm.

He sits down too.

ADA goes for more plates.

ROBERT rolls his sleeves up. He has a tattoo on his arm.

ADA returns and puts their plates down.

ADA: Robert.

ROBERT: Yes?

She rubs her own arm.

Oh.

He quickly rolls his sleeve down.

AISHA cuts into her steak.

AISHA: It's all bloody.

ADA: Yes, it's lovely, isn't it?

AISHA and NICHOLAE try to eat the food. They are revolted by it.

ROBERT: Mmmmmmm.

ADA: Mmmmmmmmmmmmmmmmmm. Tasty.

ROBERT: Mmmmmmmmmmmmmmmmmmmmmmmmmmmm. Very juicy.

Blood starts to drip down ADA's chin.

ADA: Ooops.

ROBERT chuckles.

ADA giggles and wipes the blood away daintily.

When they're not looking, NICHOLAE puts the meat in his pocket. AISHA watches him.

ROBERT: Okay?

ADA: Yes.

NICHOLAE: (*Pointing to the ceiling.*) Look!

ADA: What?

NICHOLAE: There's a fly up there.

ADA: I can't see it.

NICHOLAE: Yes!

He indicates to AISHA that she should put the meat in her pocket.

ROBERT: I like flies.

ADA: Robert!

ROBERT: Oh! Sorry!

AISHA has put the meat in her pocket.

ADA: Goodness me! You've both finished. Do you want some more?

NICH/AISH: No thank you.

NICHOLAE: Can we leave the table?

ROBERT: We don't expect you to eat it.

NICHOLAE: What?

ADA: Oh Robert! (*She laughs.*) You said, 'Can we leave the table?' and he said, 'We don't expect you to eat it!' Do you understand?

NICHOLAE: No.

ADA: Well, you'd say, 'Can I leave the cabbage?' wouldn't you, if you didn't want to eat it?

NICHOLAE: Yes.

ADA: So Robert said, 'We don't expect you to eat the table!'

NICHOLAE: Right.

ADA laughs.

Can we?

ADA: Of course you can.

AISHA and NICHOLAE go.

ADA and ROBERT watch them.

ROBERT: Did they eat it?

ADA: No, they put it in their pockets.

ROBERT: Hmmmm. Is there really a fly up there?

ADA: No that was just to distract us.

ROBERT: Clever boy.

ADA: Yes.

They continue eating.

Sound of toilet flushing.

Scene 3

NICHOLAE is looking at a photo album. AISHA enters.

AISHA: It turned the water in the toilet pink.

NICHOLAE: So did mine.

AISHA: It was disgusting. I'm going to tell Mum.

NICHOLAE: Her door's locked.

AISHA: I'll knock.

NICHOLAE: She's not answering.

AISHA sits down beside him.

I'm sure I've seen them somewhere before.

AISHA: Did you see his arm? He had that thing on it.

NICHOLAE: It's a tattoo.

AISHA: It was a skellington.

NICHOLAE: A skull. And did you see what it said underneath?

AISHA: No.

NICHOLAE: It said D-E-A-T-H.

AISHA: Dee Ath.

NICHOLAE: Death! It said DEATH!

AISHA: I don't like them.

NICHOLAE: (*Indicating a photo in the album.*) There!

AISHA: What?

NICHOLAE: Look!

He shows her a photo.

It's them. See?

AISHA: Who's the little girl with them?

NICHOLAE: I don't know.

AISHA: There's writing on the back.

NICHOLAE turns it over.

NICHOLAE: It's Mum's writing.

AISHA: What does it say?

NICHOLAE: 'My time in hell!'

They look at each other.

Suddenly ADA is behind them.

ADA: You two should be getting ready for bed.

NICHOLAE hides the photo.

AISHA: I want to see Mum.

ADA: Not tonight, darling.

AISHA: Why not?

ADA: Because she's not herself.

NICHOLAE: What do you mean?

ADA: Pardon?

NICHOLAE: What do you mean, she's not herself?

ADA: I just mean she needs a rest. Now, go on.

AISHA and NICHOLAE go.

ADA picks up the photo album and looks through it.

ROBERT enters.

There's their mother when she was little. You remember her?

ROBERT: I remember.

ADA: And there she is with her parents, my dear brother and that silly wife he married. Look at him. You can see how weak he is!

ROBERT: He tasted nice though.

ADA: Shhh!

Scene 4

AISHA and NICHOLAE are in their pyjamas.

AISHA: Can you hear them?

NICHOLAE: No.

AISHA: Do you think they've gone to bed?

NICHOLAE: They're not in the spare room, I looked.

AISHA: Maybe really they're robbers.

NICHOLAE: We haven't got anything worth robbing.

AISHA: We've got the video.

NICHOLAE: It's really old, that video.

AISHA: Maybe Ada's a witch.

NICHOLAE: Don't be silly.

Hissing sound.

AISHA: What was that?

NICHOLAE: It was probably just the water pipes.

Hissing sound again.

Maybe –

AISHA: What?

NICHOLAE: Maybe I could go downstairs.

AISHA: What for?

NICHOLAE: I want to look in the fridge.

AISHA: What for?

NICHOLAE: I don't know.

AISHA: I'm coming too.

NICHOLAE: You have to be quiet.

AISHA: I know.

NICHOLAE: I'm going to open the door. Put the light off.

She turns off the light.

Do you think we should?

AISHA: Yes.

The hissing noise is louder and something long and slithery goes across the stage.

What was that?

NICHOLAE: It looked like…

AISHA: What?

NICHOLAE: A snake.

AISHA: Where did it go?

NICHOLAE: It disappeared into the wall.

He opens the door a bit wider and it creaks.

Shhh.

ADA: What's going on?

The children scream and turn.

ROBERT is standing right behind them.

They scream again.

What are you doing? Eh? Where are you going?

NICHOLAE: We uh…

ADA: Yes?

NICHOLAE: We…

ADA: You what?

NICHOLAE: We're…

AISHA: We're thirsty. Can we have a drink of water?

ADA: Of course.

She goes.

ROBERT looks at them.

ROBERT: Booh.

He laughs at his own humour.

ADA: Here you are. Now get some sleep.

The children take the glasses and go.

How's it going in there?

ROBERT: She's resisting.

ADA: Has Mephista – ?

ROBERT: She's working on it.

ADA: The gateway's closing. We haven't got much time.

ROBERT looks towards where AISHA and NICHOLAE have gone.

ROBERT: I'm hungry.

ADA: Robert!

ROBERT: Those kids look so appetising.

ADA: You can't. You'd ruin everything.

ROBERT: I know.

Hissing sound.

ADA: Go on!

Scene 5

NICHOLAE is in bed dreaming.

NICHOLAE: Help! Mum! Help! No! Help!

AISHA enters. She has a notebook in her hand.

AISHA: Nicholae!

NICHOLAE: No!

AISHA: Nicholae!

NICHOLAE: I'm falling! I'm falling!

AISHA: Nicholae! Wake up!

NICHOLAE: What? Oh! I was falling. They were chasing me and I fell over a cliff in the snow.

AISHA: Mum's gone.

NICHOLAE: What?

AISHA: I went into her room and she wasn't there.

NICHOLAE: Perhaps she's downstairs.

AISHA: I've got her book. Look!

NICHOLAE: What?

AISHA: It's full of scribbles. I can't read it.

He takes the book.

NICHOLAE: 'Beyond the rift.' 'The One Who Wears the Deathly Crown – Dietrich. Angry. Wants to come back.' Ummm. 'Feeds on fear, it makes him strong. But he doesn't know where the Gateways are.' Can't read the next bit. 'The Gateway's forming, I can feel it. Will they come through.' Question mark, question mark.

AISHA: What's a Gateway?

NICHOLAE: It's all mad stuff that she's got in her head.

AISHA: It's not mad.

NICHOLAE: She's ill, Aisha. Because Dad left.

AISHA: She's not.

She grabs the notebook and turns to go.

NICHOLAE: Where are you going?

AISHA: I'm going to find Mum.

NICHOLAE: You can't go downstairs.

AISHA: Why not?

NICHOLAE: Because they're down there.

AISHA: So? You think they're okay. You think Mum's mad. If she's mad then there's nothing to be scared about.

She starts to go downstairs.

NICHOLAE: Aisha.

She ignores him.

He follows her onto the landing.

Aisha!

She starts to go down the stairs.

AISHA: Ugh.

NICHOLAE: What?

AISHA: There's all slimy stuff on the stairs like when the slugs get into the front room and leave their trail on the carpet.

They bend down and look at it.

Hissing sound.

What was that?

NICHOLAE: It came from the kitchen.

They start to creep down again.

ADA: Look at the light under the kitchen door.

NICHOLAE: There's smoke.

He moves closer.

AISHA: Are you going to open the door?

He doesn't answer.

I'm scared.

He doesn't answer.

Are you?

NICHOLAE: No.

He reaches out for the door.

They put their hands up to their eyes because they are blinded by the light.

AISHA: It's so bright.

NICHOLAE: It's coming from the fridge.

AISHA: I can't see anything.

NICHOLAE: Look.

AISHA: Where?

NICHOLAE: In the back of the fridge.

AISHA: What is it?

NICHOLAE: That's where the light is.

AISHA: Maybe it's a gateway.

NICHOLAE: There's no such thing.

AISHA: Come on.

She grabs his hand.

NICHOLAE: We can't go into the fridge.

AISHA: Why not?

NICHOLAE: We might get shut in.

AISHA: But that might be where Mum is.

They look.

NICHOLAE: You think we should?

AISHA: Of course. We have to.

They walk into the light.

NICHOLAE: It's cold.

AISHA: It's freezing.

They pass some fish fingers. And a bag of peas.

Change of sound.

They are on the top of a mountain.

Scene 6

The top of the mountain.

AISHA: Where are we?

NICHOLAE: We're very high up.

AISHA: Do you think we're beyond the rift?

NICHOLAE: I don't know.

AISHA: My feet are cold.

A silvery animal (THEODORE) stands on its hind legs to look at them.

Look! Over there in the snow.

The animal indicates that they should follow it.

THEODORE:
Follow me through the snow
down the mountainside we go.
up there in the clear blue sky
something's watching with eagle eye.

Danger hovers all around
not much life here to be found
all the animals have left
and there's only fear and death.

AISH/NICH:
Where's this leading?
where's this going?
all this toing?
all this froing?
what's this world
so cold and white?
what will happen
in the night?
what's this path?
what's this song?
wish I had
my jumper on.
in a place
as cold as this,
some nice warm shoes
wouldn't go amiss.

THEODORE:
Soon we'll reach the ancient wood
the magic place of childhood.

it's always winter there as well
as if it's under some dark spell.

but never fear stay positive
or else you'll lose your will to live
just remember that you must
keep your faith in her you trust.

AISHA: Look, Nicholae!

NICHOLAE: What?

AISHA: In the snow. Isn't that…?

NICHOLAE picks up a key.

NICHOLAE: It's the key Mum keeps in the dish on her
dressing table.

AISHA: What's it doing here?

NICHOLAE: I don't know.

AISHA: She must have come this way.

*The silver animal indicates that they should carry on. He
waves to them.*

THEODORE:
Now my little task is done
now I'm sorry I have to run.
others will help you on your way
how it ends I cannot say.

He waves and goes.

AISHA and NICHOLAE hear snoring.

*The GUARDIAN (Behan) is asleep at the entrance to the
forest.*

AISHA: We could ask him if he's seen Mum.

NICHOLAE: Hello!

The GUARDIAN snores.

NICHOLAE: Hey!

GUARDIAN: Mmmmm?

He snores again.

AISHA: Hey!

He continues to snore.

NICHOLAE touches him.

He jumps and looks all around him and doesn't see the children. He calms down and turns to sit down again when he sees them and jumps.

GUARDIAN: Who are you?

AISHA: Who are you?

GUARDIAN: I asked first.

NICHOLAE: I'm Nicholae and this is Aisha.

GUARDIAN: I see.

AISHA: So who are you?

GUARDIAN: I'm Behan, the guardian of the forest.

AISHA: But you were asleep.

GUARDIAN: I was not asleep! How dare you!

NICHOLAE: Have you seen our Mum?

GUARDIAN: What's a Mum?

AISHA: It's someone who looks after you. A grown up person.

GUARDIAN: I had one of those once, I think when we lived beyond the –

NICHOLAE: What?

AISHA: Beyond the rift?

GUARDIAN: I can't tell you. I shouldn't have said. He'll be angry.

AISHA: Who'll be angry?

GUARDIAN: Shhh.

AISHA: Is it the One Who Wears the Deathly Crown?

Distant roaring.

GUARDIAN: Shhh. Who told you about him?

AISHA: My Mum. Look she wrote about it in –

NICHOLAE kicks her.

Aowhh.

NICHOLAE: Have you seen her? She's about this tall and she's got black hair.

AISHA: And she's got a mole on her arm just here.

GUARDIAN: No-one's been past here for days.

AISHA: But they could have gone past while you were sleeping.

GUARDIAN: How many times do I have to tell you? I was not sleeping. I never sleep.

NICHOLAE: Maybe she's in the forest.

GUARDIAN: Well, I don't fancy her chances if she is.

AISHA: Why not?

GUARDIAN: Because nothing that goes into that forest comes back to tell the tale.

AISHA: Why not?

GUARDIAN: Because

He looks round.

Because She Who Was Here Before lives in there, that's why.

AISHA: Who's She Who Was Here Before?

GUARDIAN: (*Mouths.*) Mephista.

NICHOLAE: What?

GUARDIAN: (*Mouths louder.*) Mephista.

NICHOLAE: Mephista?

GUARDIAN: Shhhhh.

Hissing noise.

Be careful. If you get scared you'll call her out and she'll turn herself into your greatest fear. And once she knows what you fear she climbs into your head and steals your will.

AISHA: Your will? What's that? I don't know if I've got one.

GUARDIAN: Oh you've got one alright. Everyone has a will until they meet (*He mouths.*) Mephista. This was her world, before we came here. Now she serves Dietrich, The One.

AISHA: But we have to find our Mum.

GUARDIAN: Well, if you're going in there, just make sure you don't get scared. Now, I can't stay chatting to you. I've already told you more than I should. I have to get on with my work. It's very hard work being a guardian, you know. And don't you go telling anyone stories about me sleeping on the job either.

NICHOLAE: We won't.

GUARDIAN: It's that way.

NICHOLAE: Thank you.

GUARDIAN: Bye.

AISH/NICH: Goodbye.

The GUARDIAN falls asleep.

AISHA: It's getting dark.

NICHOLAE looks up.

What are we going to do?

NICHOLAE: Find Mum.

AISHA: So do you think we should go in there?

NICHOLAE: Of course we should.

They enter the wood.

Sound of the wood – hissing sound of MEPHISTA.

Scene 7

In the wood.

AISHA: Can you see anything?

NICHOLAE gets out Mum's diary.

What was that?

NICHOLAE: It was just the wind in the dead leaves.

AISHA: I'm scared.

NICHOLAE: Don't be. You heard what he said. Listen to this, 'Mephista – bad bad bad. She was there before. She kept the Deathly Crown buried deep underground.

Dietrich crossed over and tricked her. He became the One. They had children together. The Flesheaters.'

AISHA: Can you smell…?

NICHOLAE: What?

AISHA: I thought I could…

NICHOLAE: Yes.

AISHA: It's what Mum smells like when she gets out of the bath.

NICHOLAE: It's her special soap.

AISHA: She must be near.

NICHOLAE: Yes.

They curl up.

Sound of the wind in the dead leaves and branches.

Hissing.

NICHOLAE is dreaming.

No. I'm falling! No!

AISHA wakes.

AISHA: (*Whispering.*) Nicholae! Shhh!

Hissing louder.

Nicholae, shhh. It's there.

NICHOLAE: I was falling and I got scared.

AISHA: Nicholae, I can see –

NICHOLAE: It's a dark dark hole.

AISHA: Leave me alone!

NICHOLAE: It goes down and down forever.

AISHA: Nicholae, there's Kiera and Sally and they're laughing at me.

NICHOLAE: And I'm going to fall.

AISHA: They're saying I smell.

NICHOLAE: Aisha, we mustn't get scared.

AISHA: We could sing Rusty Car.

NICHOLAE: That's for babies.

AISHA: Now they're pulling faces at me.

NICHOLAE: Empty your mind.

AISHA: What?

NICHOLAE: It's what I used to do when Mum and Dad were rowing. You know, before he left. I used to look at the light in the street and if I really concentrated I could stop hearing what Mum and Dad were saying and I could stop thinking and I wasn't scared any more. Close your eyes!

AISHA: They won't sit beside me.

NICHOLAE: Close your eyes!

She does so.

Imagine the street light outside our window. Can you see it?

AISHA: I think so. The boys are holding their noses and pointing.

NICHOLAE: Now just see the rays of light. There are like tiny particles of light.

AISHA: What are particles?

NICHOLAE: Like little flies made up of light.

AISHA: I can see them.

NICHOLAE: Just let them fill your mind.

AISHA: Okay. Now Miss MacKendrick's laughing at me too.

NICHOLAE: See the light, Aisha. The light, the light.

AISHA: The light, the light.

NICHOLAE: The light the light.

AISHA: The light the light.

The hissing gets quieter as the two children chant. Their chanting fades away too.

Silence.

They open their eyes.

Has she gone?

NICHOLAE: I think so.

AISHA: Was that her? Mephista?

NICHOLAE: Yes.

AISHA: It was like the thing we saw on the landing.

NICHOLAE: I know.

AISHA: Do you think she's got Mum?

NICHOLAE: She might have.

AISHA: What are we going to do?

NICHOLAE: Follow her.

AISHA: Follow her?

NICHOLAE: Yes. She went that way.

AISHA: You think we should?

NICHOLAE: We have to.

They leave.

Scene 8

MEPHISTA:
    I ruled this world
    when time unfurled
    and this universe was born.
    and I brought with me the Deathly Crown
    from the stars above
    down down down
    and I buried it here
    deep underground
    I became the fear
    of every creature here.
    I petrified them
    then crept inside them
    to steal their wills:
    their will to live
    their will to survive
    their will to eat
    their will to strive
    their will to laugh
    their will to cry
    and all that was left
    was their will to die.
    In this way
    they became my prey
    unable to run away
    and I devoured them
    a little bit each day.
    But then he came
    the One
    the One
    and he flattered me

and he gave me sons
flesheating ones,
and I trusted him
and I took him down
down under the ground
and I showed him the Crown.
and gave it to him
and became his slave.
I'll steal your will and deliver you
to my master who
will milk your body of your fear.
Fear is his food
and fear gives him power
and day by day
and hour by hour
he grows stronger and stronger.
and soon he'll cross over,
there will be life
no longer.

She speaks to the earth.

Yash taa yash tow yash taw.

She passes through.

NICHOLAE and AISHA enter.

AISHA: She's disappeared.

NICHOLAE: Look at this, it's like a nest.

AISHA: I've never seen eggs like that.

NICHOLAE: They're like dinosaur'zs eggs.

AISHA: What are we going to do?

NICHOLAE: Keep following her.

AISHA: Into the ground?

NICHOLAE: Yes.

AISHA: How?

NICHOLAE: Hold my hand.

They hold hands.

Yash taa yash tow yash taw.

Sound of doors sliding open.

Come on! Quick!

They pass through.

Sound of doors sliding shut.

AISHA: It's dark.

NICHOLAE: Of course it is. We're in the ground.

AISHA: I'm getting sc –

NICHOLAE: Don't. She's not far ahead. She'll smell your fear.

AISHA: Ughhh.

NICHOLAE: What?

AISHA: I trod on something.

NICHOLAE: What is it?

AISHA: It's all covered in slime.

NICHOLAE: Don't get scared.

AISHA: I'm trying.

NICHOLAE: Let's see.

AISHA: It's disgusting.

NICHOLAE looks at the slime – there is a little light inside it.

NICHOLAE: Mmmm. Look there's like a light inside it.

AISHA: Do you think she dropped it?

NICHOLAE: I don't know.

AISHA: Maybe it's somebody's will. Do you think it is?

NICHOLAE: How should I know? I've never seen anyone's will.

The light goes out.

It's gone out.

AISHA: Is it dead?

He shrugs.

Do you think it's got Mum's will?

NICHOLAE: Come on!

AISHA: There's someone coming.

Sound of voices.

The children hide.

VOICES: Down, down, down, we go. We have no will. We have no will.

1: I'm an old lady who was scared of dying.

2: I'm a little girl who's scared of the dark.

3: I was scared of the boss.

4: I was scared that the other boys would find out I played with my sister's dolls.

5: I was scared of being fat.

6: I was scared of being thin.

7: I was a child scared of the teacher.

8: I was a teacher scared of the children.

9: I was a soldier scared of getting killed.

10: I was a doctor scared of getting ill.

ALL: Down, down, down we go. We have no choice. We have to follow, we have no will.

They pass.

AISHA and NICHOLAE emerge.

AISHA: They were like ghosts.

NICHOLAE: They were like Mum.

AISHA: Nicholae?

NICHOLAE: What?

AISHA: Do you think this is a dream?

NICHOLAE: What do you mean?

AISHA: Do you think it's like one of those stories where the children wake up and find themselves back in bed and it's all been a dream?

NICHOLAE: It can't be, can it?

AISHA: Why not?

NICHOLAE: Because in dreams you never get anyone saying this is only a dream.

AISHA: How do you know?

NICHOLAE: Because I've tried that. Every night before I go to sleep.

AISHA: Tried what?

NICHOLAE: Well, you know my nightmares?

AISHA: Yes.

NICHOLAE: I thought if I could remember to tell myself that it's only a dream while I am actually dreaming then I wouldn't be scared of falling into the black hole.

AISHA: Didn't it work?

NICHOLAE: No. I never remember to say it when I'm in the nightmare.

AISHA: So this isn't a dream?

NICHOLAE: I don't think so. Come on. I can see something up ahead. It looks like the tunnel is getting bigger.

Sound of water dripping.

AISHA: Wow!

NICHOLAE: It's a lake.

AISHA: Under the ground.

The second GUARDIAN (Cepar) meets them – he looks the same as Behan.

GUARDIAN: Hello. Lost your wills, have you? This way. My boat's just over there. Now, you know the form, you have to give me the last warmth in your bodies and in return I'll row you across to the palace.

AISHA: What are you doing here?

GUARDIAN: What do you mean?

AISHA: I thought you were the guardian of the forest.

GUARDIAN: Oh you've met my brother Behan, have you? That lazy bones. Bet he was sleeping on the job. Was he?

AISHA: Well…

NICHOLAE: No.

GUARDIAN: Mmmm. Well, I'm not him. I'm Cepar, the Guardian of the Lake. There have been lots of you this morning. Sad. So pathetic, they are. And they all think they're coming back. But they never do. Come on, let's get in the boat.

AISHA: Just a minute.

GUARDIAN: I beg your pardon?

AISHA: You can't just tell us what to do without explaining anything. Lots of who?

GUARDIAN: The ones who've lost their wills of course.

NICHOLAE: And what palace?

GUARDIAN: Hang on, hang on. You're asking a lot of questions. Are you sure you've lost your wills?

AISH/NICH: No.

GUARDIAN: No?

NICHOLAE: We haven't lost anything.

GUARDIAN: You haven't?

AISHA: Except our Mum. We're looking for her.

GUARDIAN: Your Mum?

AISHA: Have you seen her?

GUARDIAN: Oh my dizzy uncle! Rattle my planks. Two children, a boy and a girl, still with their wills coming to look for their Mum. I never thought…

NICHOLAE: What?

GUARDIAN: Amos said you would come one day.

AISHA: Who's Amos?

GUARDIAN: You're the son and daughter of the one with the gift.

NICHOLAE: Are we?

GUARDIAN: I heard she was back, they've captured her again. But I thought it was just rumours. Is it true?

AISHA: Are you talking about our Mum?

GUARDIAN: So brave. The first time, she was only a child and she held out against them for so long. Dietrich couldn't use her gift unless she gave in. Then she escaped, of course.

AISHA: Is Dietrich the One Who Wears the Deathly Crown?

Roaring sound. Louder than before.

GUARDIAN: Shhhhhh. He'll hear you!

AISHA: (*Holding the notebook.*) Mum wrote about him.

GUARDIAN: Why has she come back? She shouldn't have let them bring her back. What happened to her over there?

NICHOLAE: Over there?

GUARDIAN: In the world beyond the rift.

AISHA: You mean in our world?

GUARDIAN: The world where people have birthdays and Christmas and holidays and outings and sausages and chips and chocolate chip ice cream. Is that where you're from?

AISHA: Yes.

GUARDIAN: Then you are from over there.

NICHOLAE: Yes, we are.

GUARDIAN: And you are the children of the one with the gift.

AISHA: What gift?

GUARDIAN: The gift that was given to her ancestors. The gift of being able to sense when a gateway is opening that leads from one world to the next. If Dietrich can get that then he'll be able to cross over into all the different worlds.

NICHOLAE: Is that what he wants?

GUARDIAN: He wants to destroy all life. Oh, Dietrich!

Pause.

NICHOLAE: Do you know Ada?

AISHA: And Robert?

GUARDIAN: Does he bear the mark?

AISHA: He's got a skull on his arm.

GUARDIAN: Yes. The Flesheater. Son of The One. And Ada who brought her over last time. Her aunt.

AISHA: We think they took Mum.

GUARDIAN: Yes. I'm afraid it must have happened. She is probably already in the Palace of The One.

AISHA: We have to find her.

GUARDIAN: Yes.

NICHOLAE: So will you take us across?

GUARDIAN: I'm not allowed to take anyone across without them paying me.

AISHA: We haven't got anything.

GUARDIAN: Hmmm. Let me see. Now there is something, something that I've heard about but never seen. If you could show it to me then I'm sure that technically I could accept it as payment.

NICHOLAE: What is it?

GUARDIAN: I don't know what it's called but I've heard about it. It's something you people do. You stretch your lips and open your mouths and then you start to pant and make a funny sort of noise like huh huh huh huh and sometimes water comes out of your eyes but it's supposed to be a very nice feeling. One of the ones without wills told me that it's the best medicine. But none of them can remember how to do it by the time they get to me. Do you know what it is?

AISHA: Is it crying?

NICHOLAE: That's not a nice feeling.

AISHA: Sometimes I like crying.

NICHOLAE: I think I know what it is. Is it laughter?

GUARDIAN: That's it! That's it! Can you laughter for me?

AISHA: (*Giggling.*) You don't laughter. You laugh.

GUARDIAN: You're doing it! You're doing it!

He tries to copy her which makes both the children laugh.

AISHA: (*Laughing and waving her arms.*) No! No, that's not right.

CEPAR mimics her.

GUARDIAN: No, no, that's not right.

This makes AISHA and NICHOLAE laugh more.

Yes! Yes! Go on!

He tries to copy them which again makes them laugh.

Oh, what a funny thing, I'm almost forgetting I'm sad.

He copies their laughter which they find even funnier.

Oh dear! I think I can safely say that you've given me ample payment.

He laughs again.

NICHOLAE and AISHA laugh.

Oh, but there's just one thing. The Palace of the One has many rooms.

NICHOLAE and AISHA are still laughing.

AISHA: (*Still laughing.*) Like dining rooms and ballrooms?

NICHOLAE: (*Still laughing.*) And toilets?

GUARDIAN: No.

Their laughter subsides.

NICHOLAE: No?

GUARDIAN: No. Each of the hundreds of rooms contains a different fear.

AISHA: A fear.

GUARDIAN: And if you enter the room of your greatest fear then you never get out again. And your mother could be in any of them. You might look for years and never find her.

He laughs but sees they are no longer laughing.

Oh, the nice feeling has gone. Do it again.

NICHOLAE and AISHA look at him.

Why won't you do it?

NICHOLAE: We can't.

GUARDIAN: Why not?

NICHOLAE: Because things don't seem funny any more.

GUARDIAN: I see. Do you still want to go across?

NICHOLAE: (*To AISHA.*) Do you think we should?

AISHA: We have to.

GUARDIAN: Hop in, then.

Scene 9

They are standing in a great cavern, looking up and round. Sound of a machine – like a giant milking machine.

AISHA: So many doors.

NICHOLAE: They just lead into the rock.

AISHA: Mum might be in any of them.

NICHOLAE: We'll just have to open all of them.

AISHA: And that noise.

NICHOLAE: It's some sort of machine.

AISHA: What's this for?

She is looking at a glass dial.

NICHOLAE: It's a meter.

AISHA: The needle's pointing to full.

He taps it.

Look, the doors have got writing on them.

She tries to read.

Agor…agora…agorap…

NICHOLAE: Agoraphobia – it means that you're scared of going outside. This one says hydrophobia, that's fear of water.

AISHA: There's a really little door down here.

She bends down and opens it.

The sound of the milking machine gets louder.

Hello!

NICHOLAE: Aisha!

AISHA: What?

NICHOLAE: Be careful.

AISHA: Is there anyone there?

CLAUSTROPHOBE: Hello?

AISHA: Oh hello. What's your name?

CLAUSTROPHOBE: I'm Henry.

AISHA: How old are you?

CLAUSTROPHOBE: I'm nine. Not that it's any of your business. Now can you close that door, please?

AISHA: Why?

CLAUSTROPHOBE: Because this is meant to be the room for people with claustrophobia.

AISHA: What's that?

CLAUSTROPHOBE: It's for people who don't like being shut in small spaces so if you open the door then it's no longer a confined space.

AISHA: But is our Mum there?

CLAUSTROPHOBE: There's no-one else in here but me. There's not room for anyone else. Now close the door.

AISHA: Alright.

She closes the door. The milking machine sound gets softer.

Did you see?

NICHOLAE: What?

AISHA: He had that all those tubes coming out of him going into the wall.

NICHOLAE: Yes. It was like –

AISHA: Like what?

NICHOLAE: Like when we went on that trip to the farm and we watched the cows being milked. The milk got sucked out of the cows and went through the pipes and ended up in a big tank. That had a dial on it like this.

AISHA: (*Going to another door.*) What does this one say?

NICHOLAE: Arachnophobia – I think that's fear of spiders.

AISHA: Ugggh.

NICHOLAE: Hey!

AISHA: What?

NICHOLAE: Mum doesn't like spiders. She always gets Dad to take them outside.

AISHA: When he was there.

NICHOLAE: Maybe he's put her in there.

AISHA: Who? The One Who Wears the Deathly Crown?

Louder roaring.

NICHOLAE: Don't say his name!

The roaring subsides.

We'd better look.

He goes to open the door.

AISHA: I think I'm a bit scared of spiders too.

NICHOLAE opens the door. Sound of hundreds of spider legs crawling (and milking machine?).

Ugghhh. There are hundreds of them. Spiders! And they're crawling all over the people.

NICHOLAE: Excuse me!

AISHA: Let's go.

NICHOLAE: Hello!

AISHA: Come on Nicholae, I don't like it in here.

NICHOLAE: Hello! Excuse me! Can you help?

ARACHNOPHOBE: Hello, you want to come in? There are bigger ones over the other side. In the corner over there, there's a hole and a huge one lives in there. She's got great big hairy legs and she creeps up on you when you're not looking and wraps you in her threads. It's really horrible.

AISHA: Ughh.

NICHOLAE: Have you seen our Mum?

ARACHNOPHOBE: Oh look! I think I can see a leg. She's coming out of her hole! She must know that you've arrived. Can you see? She can move really fast when she wants to. She scuttles across the floor and the very sight of her makes you shiver with fright. Look she's coming!

AISHA: Nicholae!

NICHOLAE: Why don't you leave then?

ARACHNOPHOBE: What?

NICHOLAE: The door's not locked you could leave at any time.

ARACHNOPHOBE: Leave?

NICHOLAE: Yes.

ARACHNOPHOBE: I have to stay here.

NICHOLAE: Why?

ARACHNOPHOBE: Because this is my place.

AISHA: Do you like spiders?

ARACHNOPHOBE: Of course not. I'm terrified of them.

AISHA: So let's go. Come on.

NICHOLAE: Let me help. I'll take those funny tubes off you.

He reaches out to pull the suckers off her.

She slaps his hand.

ARACHNOPHOBE: Go away!

NICHOLAE: Aowh.

ARACHNOPHOBE: Leave me in peace! Don't you understand anything? When you're really terrified of something then you hold on to your fear like it's the most precious thing in your life. You're so afraid that you can't let it go.

NICHOLAE: But the door's just over there.

ARACHNOPHOBE: Who do you think you are? Coming in here, interfering?

AISHA: We're only looking for our Mum.

ARACHNOPHOBE: Well, she's not in here. Oh look, she's coming for me. Oh…ohhhhh…I'm terrified.

A big brown leg reaches out for AISHA who screams and runs.

They manage to get outside and close the door.

The sound of the milking machine gets softer and the spiders stop.

AISHA: That was horrible. Why doesn't she just leave? She must want to really.

NICHOLAE: But that's the point. Don't you see?

AISHA: What?

NICHOLAE: She has no will. When you have no will then you can't do what you want to do. The One has got her will.

Roaring sound.

AISHA: (*Whispering.*) Do you think that's him?

NICHOLAE: I think it must be.

AISHA: It's like a lion.

NICHOLAE: It sounds bigger than a lion.

AISHA: There are so many rooms. We'll never find Mum.

NICHOLAE: Shhh!

AISHA: What?

NICHOLAE: There's someone coming. Quick hide.

They hide.

ROBERT and ADA enter.

ADA: Come on, Robert, he needs his dinner.

ROBERT: I need my dinner.

ADA: Stop complaining. He hates that.

ROBERT: Why did he give me a will, if he doesn't want me to complain?

ADA: Just think what it will be like when he's strong enough to cross over. He'll march into the worlds beyond the rift and you'll be captain of his army of Flesheaters.

ROBERT: If he gets the Gift from your niece. If she doesn't escape again.

ADA: She won't escape this time. Now give me the spanner.

She starts to drain off fear from the Arachnophobia room.

ROBERT: You could at least have let me eat up her two children. He wouldn't have known about it.

ADA: How many times do I have to tell you? He needed to find out if they have the Gift. If they followed us then he'll know that one or both of them can sense the Gateways.

ROBERT: You think they're here somewhere?

ADA: If they've crossed over, we'll find them. Right that should do.

She turns off the tap.

ROBERT: Yuk, don't know how he can eat this stuff. Give me a nice bit of meat any day.

ADA: He's waiting, Robert.

They go.

NICHOLAE and AISHA come out from their hiding place.

AISHA: You see? Everything she wrote in the notebook is true about the Gateways and about the One.

NICHOLAE: Mmmm.

AISHA: Nicholae?

NICHOLAE: What?

AISHA: Do you think you've got the Gift?

NICHOLAE: No.

AISHA: But you felt something by the fridge.

NICHOLAE: No I didn't.

Beat.

AISHA: Come on!

NICHOLAE: Where?

AISHA: We have to follow them.

NICHOLAE: Why?

AISHA: To find out where Mum is.

Roars.

NICHOLAE: You think we should?

AISHA: We have to.

They go.

Scene 10

The roaring gets louder. ROBERT and ADA scurry in with the bucket and spoons. There is a great mouth. There are bottles with little lights in them – the wills stolen by MEPHISTA which have not yet been given to Flesheaters. They start spooning fear from the bucket into THE ONE's mouth. The roaring stops.

THE ONE: More.

ADA: Yes, your Highness.

ROBERT: This comes from the Spider room Great Father.

THE ONE roars.

ADA: Oh but your Majesty it's really thick and gooey, we thought you'd like it.

ROBERT: Perhaps you'd like a nice leg of child instead Your Magnificence.

THE ONE roars.

I'm sorry, it was just an idea.

ADA: We could…

Interrogative roar.

We could see if the Room of Loneliness has produced any essence of fear, your Lordship.

Loud extended roars.

ADA and ROBERT cower subserviently.

You're quite right, Your Wickedness, we did let her escape last time. But we've got her back for you now and soon you will cross over and destroy every Universe in all times.

Pacified roar.

There are some baby Flesheaters in Mephista's nest in the forest, Your Viciousness, do you want me to go up and give them each a will?

Affirmative roar.

ROBERT: Oh goody, some brothers and sister. I'll do it, Daddy.

Angry roar.

I'm sorry.

Angry roar.

Yes I did. But it's just that they look so tasty when they first hatch out before they get their wills, I couldn't help taking a little bite.

Angry roar.

Yes, I'll let Ada do it.

ADA has been gathering some bottles.

ADA: (*Holding one up.*) What about this one, your Nastiness? It belongs to my niece.

Angry roar.

Yes of course, you're saving that one for a special purpose.

NICHOLAE enters.

NICHOLAE: Give me that!

He grabs the bottle from ADA.

THE ONE roars.

ADA: Catch him, Robert.

ROBERT chases NICHOLAE.

This is the boy, Your Maliciousness. My niece's son. He must have the gift too.

ROBERT catches NICHOLAE and brings him to the mouth of THE ONE.

NICHOLAE: Give me back my Mum.

THE ONE laughs.

Give her back to me.

ROBERT: Can I eat him, Father?

ADA: No Robert. Now give me that bottle, boy.

She snatches it off him.

Now call Mephista so that she can discover his greatest fear. Once we have his will then we can see if he has the Gift.

ROBERT: MOTHHHHHHHHHHHERRRRRRRRRR!

Hissing sound

NICHOLAE: I'm not scared.

A snakelike presence enters.

ROBERT: What's he scared of, Great Mother?

Hissing sound.

MEPHISTA:
    scared of falling
    scared of heights
    scared of holes
    darker than night.
    your legs trembling
    your hands shake
    you quake with fear
    dear dear boy up high
    why, why
    don't you fly?
    just try, just try.
    jump, jump.
    all is waiting
    there below
    your greatest fear
    is vertigo.

NICHOLAE is terrified.

AISHA enters.

AISHA: Leave him alone. Remember the light, Nicholae. Light, light, light.

ADA: Ah, so they're both here.

AISHA: Light light light. It's not him you want, it's me. I felt the Gateway in the fridge. I'm the one with the Gift.

ADA: Get her Robert!

ROBERT reaches out for AISHA.

AISHA: Leave me alone, dogbreath.

ROBERT stops, horrified.

ROBERT: Did you hear that?

ADA: Robert!

ROBERT: She called me dogbreath.

AISHA: Your are a stinky dogbreath. It must be all the meat you eat.

ROBERT: She said it again. Ada, she called me dogbreath.

ADA: Don't be such a faintheart. What's His Mightiness, your father, going to think? She's only a child.

ROBERT: Nasty things, children, they play nasty tricks on you and this one calls you names.

AISHA: Cowardy custard.

ROBERT: Arghhhhhhh! Listen to her.

THE ONE roars.

ADA: Yes, Your Allpowerfulness. Now you, come and meet Mephista.

AISHA: Get your hands off me, rat-eyes.

ADA: That's not going to work with me.

She holds AISHA.

AISHA: I WILL not let you have my WILL.

She closes her eyes.

MEPHISTA:
Friends
you want friends
your life depends on it.
If you're without friends
when the day ends
gloom descends
and tears.
I see your fears
with clarity
your greatest dread's
unpopularity.

Hissing increases.

NICHOLAE: Light, Aisha, light!

AISHA: Light, light, light.

NICHOLAE: light, light, light.

BOTH: LIGHT, LIGHT, LIGHT!

Hissing falters.

ADA: Their wills are strong, Your Omnipotence.

Grumbling roar.

Yes, Your Masterfulness. Take him to the gaping cliff,
Robert. And I'll take her to the room of unpopularity.
That should soften them up for Mephista. We'll soon find
out which of them has the Gift.

ROBERT leads off NICHOLAE and ADA takes AISHA.

Scene 11

ADA is taking AISHA to the unpopularity room.

ADA: Oh yes, very high and mighty, very wilful. Just like your mother. But we'll soon have that out of you.

AISHA: No you won't!

ADA: Oh but we WILL.

AISHA: When my Mum finds out we're here she'll rescue us.

ADA: No she won't. She's not as strong as she was before.

AISHA: You don't know my Mum.

ADA: Yes I do. I brought her up.

AISHA: You brought her up?

ADA: Didn't she tell you? Must have thought she was protecting you.

AISHA: Protecting us from what?

ADA: The Gift, of course. The Gift that was given to our ancestors back in the mists of time. The Gift of being able to sense the Gateways and close them before anyone could cross over. My father had it.

AISHA: I don't know what you're talking about.

ADA: No, you don't do you? Because you haven't got the Gift. It's your brother that's got it, isn't it?

AISHA: No.

ADA: Can't you see, we're very alike? We're strong girls with weak puny little brothers. But they're the ones who were given the Gift.

AISHA: I'm nothing like you.

ADA: My brother didn't use it. He had fearfulness in his soul and he became an insurance salesman.

AISHA: Mum's Daddy was an insurance salesman.

ADA: Yes, he was my brother. Once our father knew I didn't have the Gift he ignored me. I was useless to him. I had to creep into his library at night and read about the Gateways in his books. My brother could have just taken me to the places where they were forming because he knew. Instead I had to spend years just hoping that a Gateway would open nearby and that I would happen to see it. It was so unfair. But one day I got lucky and I crossed over. And I found myself a father who did appreciate me.

AISHA: The One.

Distant roar.

ADA: Yes, the One. But he wanted me to go back with one of his Flesheaters to find my brother and bring him down here. For years we searched for a Gateway and by the time we did get through my silly brother had married a silly wife and they had a daughter.

AISHA: That was Mum.

ADA: Very good. And she had the Gift. I could tell. She had it stronger than her father, my dear brother. So I decided to take her back instead.

AISHA: Why didn't her Daddy stop you?

ADA: (*Laughing.*) Because he couldn't. He was too weak. Robert soon dealt with him and his wife.

AISHA: What did he do to them?

ADA: What do you think he did? He ate them of course.

AISHA is horrified.

Your Mother didn't know she had the Gift. But I did. I watched her closely. One day I saw her standing in the Garden staring into space and I knew. We pushed her through and brought her here.

AISHA: But she escaped. Just like Nicholae and me are going to escape.

ADA: Why do you want to leave here? You could stay here with me and we could help the One. You could get your brother to help him find the Gateways into all possible Universes.

AISHA: I'd never help you.

ADA: If that's how you want to it to be… Come on boys and girls. Come and get her!

VOICES: Oooh, look who it is! Smelly Aisha!

ADA: Awwwwwhh look! Already I can see you looking less confident.

VOICE: Don't sit beside her, she's got nits.

AISHA: No I haven't.

VOICE: Yes you have.

VOICE: And your knickers smell of pee.

AISHA: They don't.

VOICES:
Jingle bells, Aisha smells
worse and worse each day
everybody hold your nose
be sure to run away, hey!

AISHA: Leave me alone.

ADA: Ahhhhhhhh. Is she getting upset? Are you going to cry?

AISHA: No.

ADA: So why are there tears in your eyes?

VOICES:
Jingle bells, Aisha smells
she should be put away.
There's a pong and it's so strong
go and get the toilet spray.

ADA: Nobody likes you Aisha. They all hate you.

AISHA: That's not true.

ADA: Nobody wants to sit beside you at school. Your Daddy went away and left you.

AISHA: Shut up!

ADA: Poor little smelly Aisha. Nobody loves you.

AISHA: My Mum loves me.

ADA: Where is she? She's not here.

AISHA: My Mum loves me and my Dad loves me.

ADA: Neither of them love you.

AISHA: They do!

She starts to cry.

ADA: Mephista! She's ready for you.

Hissing.

MUM'S VOICE: Aisha!

AISHA: Mum!

MUM'S VOICE: Always remember that if people say horrible things to you it's probably because they're frightened of someone saying it to them.

AISHA: Where are you, Mum?

ADA: She's not here, Aisha.

MUM'S VOICE: Just remember they're scared, Aisha, then you won't be scared of them.

ADA: Come and get her, Mephista.

AISHA: Leave me!

The snake hisses as if it has been scalded.

ADA: She's full of fear.

AISHA: No I'm not. I'm not like you. Nobody loved you when your were a little girl.

ADA: Don't be ridiculous!

AISHA: You told me. Your Daddy loved your brother better than you.

ADA: How dare you!

AISHA: It's you that's scared of nobody loving you.

ADA: Be quiet.

AISHA:
Jingle bells, down in hell,
Ada's very cross.
She's so mad, she wants a dad
so she's made the one her boss, boss.

ADA: No! No!

The VOICES join in.

AISHA/VOICES:
Jingle bells, down in hell
Ada's very mad.
no-one thinks she's any good
and that's why she's so bad.

ADA: Mephista! What are you doing? Not me! Her!

VOICE: Ahhhhhhhhhhhhh. Poor little Ada. Daddy doesn't love her.

ADA: Leave me alone.

AISHA: Give me that bottle.

She snatches the bottle.

Goodbye, scaredy cat!

AISHA goes.

Hissing.

ADA: Now Mephista. I'm really not frightened you know. Especially now she's gone.

Hissing.

It was just a little moment but it's passed now.

Hissing.

Yes, honestly. How ridiculous to think I feel fear.

Hissing.

(*Holding up her hands.*) They're not shaking.

Hissing.

Well, just a little bit but I'm really not scared and if you could just let me pass.

Hissing.

Alright. Alright. I'll wait.

Scene 12

ROBERT is eating some meat.

ROBERT: Do you like it up here on this ledge, boy? Nice and high, isn't it? Why don't you look down? There's a lovely sheer drop beneath you. It goes on forever – just imagine! You could spend the rest of your life falling into a bottomless pit!

NICHOLAE: Leave me alone.

ROBERT: They tell me it feels like it's impossible to move when you're scared of heights. Is that true?

NICHOLAE: No.

ROBERT: So why don't you move, then?

He laughs.

You look pretty frozen to me. Are you ready for my mother yet? Eh? One of my little brothers needs a will. Shall I call her? No, I think we'll leave you with your will for a bit longer. I like to see you struggling to make yourself move and then feeling bad because you're not brave enough. So moving. So dramatic. You know I prefer eating things that have still got their wills. They try to put up a fight. It's more fun. Just watch this, boy. Go on, take a look.

He drops a bone over the cliff.

NICHOLAE looks down.

Oh the look on your face! Why don't you just jump and put an end to it all?

He laughs.

Oooh, I'm hungry. I'm always hungry. You know the only time I wasn't hungry was when I was still in my shell. Cause then I had the yolk of my mother's egg inside me. But as soon as I hatched, my father, The One, gave me a will. And I started wanting things to eat. And I've never stopped. And I – Hang on! I think I just saw a nice fat rat. Must have escaped from the fear of rodents room. Excuse me boy, I won't be long. Make sure you don't fall. And if you do, enjoy your trip!

He laughs.

Get it? Enjoy your trip!

He laughs.

Come here, ratty, ratty, ratty.

He goes.

NICHOLAE looks down.

AISHA enters.

AISHA: Nicholae!

NICHOLAE: What?

AISHA: I got away. And look!

She shows him the bottle.

Come on, we've got to find Mum. They said she was in the Room of Loneliness. Somebody must know where that is. Come on!

NICHOLAE: I can't move.

AISHA: Why not? We just have to go along the ledge and there's some steps down.

NICHOLAE: It's too far.

AISHA: You sound like…

NICHOLAE: What?

AISHA: Like them. Like the ones in the rooms. Oh no! Has she been?

NICHOLAE: Who?

AISHA: Mephista. Has she got your –

NICHOLAE: No.

AISHA: So why can't you move?

NICHOLAE: Because…

AISHA: Yes?

NICHOLAE: Because I'm petrified and that means I can't move.

AISHA: But that's just like them. That's how they get. What did she say, the spider woman? That they hold on to their fear like it's precious. That's what you're doing Nicholae. You have to let go of it.

NICHOLAE: I can't.

AISHA: You must. Here!

NICHOLAE: Don't!

She goes and takes his hand.

AISHA: Imagine that it's Mum's hand and that she's singing to you.

NICHOLAE: I can't hear her.

AISHA: She's singing Rusty Car.

NICHOLAE: She's not.

AISHA: She is.
Twinkle twinkle chocolate bar
my mum drives a rusty car –
Come on, join in.

Start the engine, pull the choke
off we go in a cloud of smoke.
Sing it Nicholae.

NICHOLAE: I can't.

AISHA: Yes you can.

She starts to lead him off the cliff.

Twinkle twinkle chocolate bar
Sing it!

NICHOLAE: My mum drives a rusty car.

AISHA: (*Prompting him.*) Start the engine

NICHOLAE: Start the engine, pull the choke.

AISHA: Off she goes in a cloud of smoke.

NICHOLAE: Don't. I can't do it, Aisha. My legs feel like
jelly and my stomach is turning.

AISHA: You can do it. You have to. For Mum. For me. I
can't rescue her without you.
Off she goes

NICHOLAE: Off she goes in a cloud of smoke

AISHA: Twinkle twinkle

NICHOLAE: chocolate bar
my mum drives a rusty car.

She has led him off the cliff.

NICHOLAE sits, shaking.

AISHA: You okay?

NICHOLAE: I think so.

AISHA: Now we just have to find the Room of Loneliness.

A little RAT has been listening.

RAT: Excuse me!

NICHOLAE: Who said that?

RAT: Me! Down here!

NICHOLAE: Oh yes!

RAT: Are you scared of me?

NICHOLAE: No.

RAT: Thank goodness for that. It's so tiring people screaming whenever they see you. Terrifying. You're not one of those Flesheaters, are you?

NICHOLAE: No.

RAT: Only there was one of them around just now. He nearly caught me but I managed to escape.

NICHOLAE: Me too.

RAT: Hate those Flesheaters. If we don't stay in the rodent room they gobble us up. So it's either staying in a room full of people screaming at you or being eaten. I mean it's not much of a choice, is it? Not much of a life. Thought I'd give it a go out here, but I'm not so sure now.

AISHA: The Flesheater is scared of children I think, so we'll protect you.

RAT: That's very kind.

AISHA: We're looking for our Mum.

RAT: Lost her will, has she?

AISHA: We think she might be in the Room of Loneliness.

RAT: I've heard about that. It's miles away from any of the other rooms.

NICHOLAE: Can you take us there?

RAT: I don't know. Maybe. One of my cousins left the rodent room to try to go there. Theodore. He thought it might be worth going there to hide from the Flesheaters. The One doesn't let anyone go there except him. Otherwise it wouldn't be a lonely place, you see.

NICHOLAE: I see.

RAT: And...

NICHOLAE: Yes?

RAT: Well, it's only rumours.

AISHA: What?

RAT: They say there's a way out there.

NICHOLAE: A way out?

RAT: A way out of the Palace of Fear. So maybe Theodore is up there having a fine old time in the houses and the barns. The only trouble is...

AISHA: What?

RAT: We can never know if he escaped. For all we know he might have got eaten as soon as he stepped outside the room.

AISHA: Will you show us the way?

RAT: Well...

ROBERT: (*Off.*) Got away from me. Drat that rat!

AISHA: He's coming back.

RAT: I think it's this way.

They go.

ROBERT enters.

ROBERT: What the – ? Where's he gone? Ada! He's got away! Ada!

Scene 13

NICHOLAE and AISHA and the RAT are standing before the mouth of THE ONE. Sound of snoring.

NICHOLAE: We can't go in there.

RAT: But that's the way Theodore said he was going to go – through the roaring cave and down the passage.

AISHA: Shhh. You'll wake him up.

NICHOLAE: It's his mouth.

RAT: Whose mouth? Just looks like a cave to me.

AISHA: Are you sure it's this way?

RAT: No, I'm not sure.

AISHA: This is where they feed him. What if they come and pour more in while we're down there?

NICHOLAE looks into the Mouth.

NICHOLAE: I can see something.

He takes out an earring.

AISHA: It's one of Mum's earrings.

RAT: You see, she must have been this way.

AISHA and NICHOLAE look at each other.

NICHOLAE: Do you think we should?

AISHA: We have to.

They approach the mouth.

AISHA: Yuk! It smells funny.

RAT: It smells of fear. I know the smell well.

They pass through the mouth.

Scene 14

NICHOLAE, AISHA and the RAT are bending down looking at a small skeleton.

RAT: Oh dear, I'm sure it's him. He had the same bone structure.

AISHA: It might not be your cousin.

RAT: Poor Theodore, he was so sure he could get out this way. He didn't know it would be so difficult. This passage goes on forever. We haven't seen a living thing for miles. Usually there's the odd bug or grub. He probably died of hunger and thirst.

NICHOLAE: Well, we're not going to do that.

AISHA: I'm tired.

NICHOLAE: We have to keep going.

Sound of gurgling.

AISHA: What's that?

Muffled satisfied roar.

NICHOLAE: He's getting fed. Oh no!

RAT: What?

AISHA: That means –

RAT: Yes?

NICHOLAE: It's coming this way!

RAT: What it?

NICHOLAE: Quick! Hold on to each other.

Gurgling gets louder.

AISHA: Ugghhhhh! I can't see anything.

NICHOLAE: Neither can I.

RAT: Nyctophobia! Nyctophobia!

NICHOLAE: What are you on about?

RAT: That's what this is. My Mother suffered from it. Fear of the dark! Most unusual for a rat. Come on, lucky for you I've got night vision.

He leads them on.

AISHA: I just want some light.

RAT: Keep going. This way.

He bumps into someone. It is the GUARDIAN, Amos.

GUARDIAN: Hey!

NICHOLAE: Hello?

GUARDIAN: Who are you?

AISHA: I recognise that voice.

GUARDIAN: Just a minute, the darkness is passing.

AISHA: It's you.

GUARDIAN: What do you mean?

AISHA: Aren't you the Guardian of the Wood?

NICHOLAE: Or maybe the Guardian of the Lake.

GUARDIAN: No, I'm Amos, the Guardian of the Inner Way. Have you met them?

AISHA: Yes.

GUARDIAN: I haven't seem them for so long. They're my brothers. They're still alive?

AISHA: Yes.

GUARDIAN: Did they seem happy?

AISHA: Well, not happy exactly. One was a bit sleepy.

GUARDIAN: Oh that's Behan, he always liked his sleep.

NICHOLAE: And the other one.

GUARDIAN: Cepar.

AISHA: We taught him how to laugh.

GUARDIAN: What's laugh?

AISHA: Well, what you do is –

RAT: Come on! Come on! Do you two want to find your Mother? Or are you going to stay here chatting forever?

AISHA: Have you seen her?

GUARDIAN: Who?

AISHA: Our Mum.

NICHOLAE: We think she's in the room of loneliness.

GUARDIAN: She's your mother?

AISHA: Yes. And we have to find her.

GUARDIAN: We had a mother once.

Roar.

No brother, everything is in order. I promise you.

Roar.

No. There's nobody down here. Nobody at all.

NICHOLAE: He's your brother too?

GUARDIAN: Yes. There were four of us. The sons of Grendel the Spirit of the Earth. There was me, I'm the youngest, Amos. Then Behan, Cepar and the eldest, Dietrich. Grendel, our mother, loved man and showed him all the wonders of the earth. And man was greedy and he got too powerful. But our Mother told us we must protect all creatures – even man. Dietrich thought she was foolish. When Man burnt down the forest and hunted us down Dietrich brought us here to escape. But he was determined to go back one day and get revenge. So our Mother gave one man the Gift so that he and his descendants could protect their world from Dietrich.

AISHA: We know about the Gift, don't we Nicholae?

NICHOLAE: No.

GUARDIAN: Dietrich tried to make us help him but when we refused he banished Behan and Cepar to the edge of our world. For a time he was good to me – I was his favourite. But when I tried to stop him creating the Flesheaters he swallowed me. He said, that way he would never be alone. So since that time I've lived down here. I haven't seen Behan and Cepar for many centuries. I miss them.

AISHA: What happened to your Mum?

GUARDIAN: She died.

NICHOLAE: How did she die?

GUARDIAN: She was poisoned.

AISHA: Poisoned?

GUARDIAN: Man poisoned the soil and the air and the rivers and the oceans and she died.

AISHA cries.

AISHA: I'm sorry.

GUARDIAN: Don't cry. You can't be held responsible for what others have done before you. Dietrich blames all of your kind. He doesn't understand that you're not all guilty. Please don't cry.

AISHA: It's so sad that you lost your Mum.

GUARDIAN: Yes. But you haven't lost yours. She's in the Room of Loneliness. That's where Dietrich puts those he treasures most. It's because they share his fear, you see. The door is just ahead. I'm not allowed to go there. But you should know that it's locked. And only Dietrich has the key. There used to be two but –

Roar.

I'm coming, brother.

Roar.

I'm coming. Farewell. Think of me sometimes.

He goes.

RAT: Well kids. I did my best. But without the key. I guess I'll have to go back to the rodent room and put up with all that screaming. Sorry.

NICHOLAE: No!

RAT: No?

NICHOLAE: We're not giving up.

He approaches the door. It has NO ENTRANCE written on it in many different languages. He tries to open it.

Mum! Mum!

AISHA: Mum!

RAT: This is useless kids. That door's so thick. Nobody could hear you through that. I'll be seeing you. Or maybe I won't.

He goes.

AISHA: Nicholae.

NICHOLAE: What?

AISHA: Try Mum's key.

NICHOLAE: Why would that fit?

AISHA: Try it.

He gets out the key they found in the snow. He puts it in the lock and turns.

The door swings open.

Do you think we should – ?

NICHOLAE: Of course.

They pass through.

Scene 15

The Room of Loneliness. MUM is sitting on the floor playing with a doll. She has tubes coming from her leading into the floor.

MUM:

Twinkle twinkle, chocolate bar
my mum drives a rusty car
start the engine, pull the choke
off we go in a puff of smoke.
Twinkle twinkle, chocolate bar
my drives a rusty car.

AISHA: Mum!

MUM: I'm not looking at you. You're not really there.

AISHA: We are here.

MUM: Don't look at them, Mary. They're just voices.

NICHOLAE: Mum?

MUM: We're not listening to you. We don't care what you do to us. Not if you try to make us eat meat. Not if you lock us in here on our own. Not if you send the snake woman to frighten us. We won't take any notice of you, will we, Mary?

AISHA: Mum, it's us. It's Nicholae and Aisha.

MUM: They're pretending to be two children just like us, Mary. We won't listen to them.

She covers her ears and the doll's ears and hums the tune of 'Twinkle Twinkle'.

AISHA: She's got the tubes on her.

NICHOLAE: I know.

AISHA takes out the bottle.

What you doing?

AISHA: I'm giving her back her will.

NICHOLAE: It won't be that easy.

MUM: Don't listen to them, Mary.

AISHA: Look, Mum.

She puts the bottle beside her.

MUM stops humming and looks at the bottle.

MUM: No, Mary, it's not meat and it's not blood. It...looks like...that thing we lost.

She takes the bottle and removes the cork and smells.

But we don't need it any more, do we Mary?

She goes to put the cork back on.

AISHA: You do need it.

She holds the bottle to her lips.

MUM: I don't want to want things. I don't want to fight.

NICHOLAE: Leave her.

AISHA: Just a little sip.

MUM: But what if they come, Mary?

She puts the doll to her ear and listens.

You think I should?

She listens again.

I'll blame you if they come.

She takes the bottle and drinks from it.

Oh, Mary it's bitter.

She drinks more.

Mary, I'm losing you.

She drinks the rest.

Gone. You've gone from me.

She closes her eyes. Pause.

AISHA: Mum?

MUM: Mmmmmm?

AISHA: Are you alright?

She opens her eyes and looks at them for the first time.

MUM: Oh no, they've got you too!

AISHA: No. We've come to find you, Mum. We came through the fridge and there was a mountain and a forest with Mephista in it but she didn't get us. And a lake and rooms with fears. And The One told Ada and Robert to put us somewhere where we'd be really scared but we escaped and then a rat brought us through The One's mouth and The One's brother, Amos, told us where you were.

MUM: Oh Nicholae, Aisha, I'm sorry.

She cries.

AISHA: Don't cry, Mum.

MUM: You can't stay here.

AISHA: We've come to take you home.

MUM: Look, there might still be time. If they don't know you're here. You must go.

AISHA: We can't go without you.

MUM: You don't need me. What use am I to you? I'm a bad mother. I can't protect you. You'll be better off without me.

AISHA: You're not a bad mother.

MUM: I am. It's because of what they did to me when I was your age. They put me in here.

NICHOLAE: But you escaped.

MUM: What?

NICHOLAE: Didn't you?

MUM: I thought I could get away from them. And I found... I found a way of getting back.

AISHA: Did you find a Gateway?

MUM: You know about the Gateways?

AISHA: Nicholae can feel them too.

NICHOLAE: Shut up, Aisha!

MUM: Oh no! He must never find out.

AISHA: Mum, come on, we can escape again.

MUM: There's no escape! I thought there was but in here (*She points to her head.*) I didn't escape. They stayed with me. For a time I was able to keep them under control. When you two were born I thought they'd gone for good. I was so happy. But then I started remembering them. I felt the Gateway forming. It's not a Gift, it's a curse. You can't fight them. That's why your Daddy left. I used to go for days without being able to talk with him. He thought I'd stopped loving him. But it was them, you see, in here. And then they came back.

AISHA: But.

MUM: Come here.

AISHA goes to her.

Nicholae?

NICHOLAE refuses.

I can't come back with you.

AISHA: Why not?

MUM: Because down here, I feel safe.

AISHA: But you're all on your own.

MUM: Yes and that's better. I don't start thinking that maybe I'm not alone.

AISHA: But you're not alone. You've got us.

MUM: Yes, but one day, you'll leave me too.

AISHA: We won't.

MUM: Just like your Daddy left me. I don't want to go through all that again. Being happy and then getting left. Down here I know where I am.

NICHOLAE: So what about us?

MUM: I...

NICHOLAE: We're meant to be the children.

MUM: I know, Nicholae.

NICHOLAE: You're meant to look after us and help us grow up. I bet you don't even know that nobody will sit next to Aisha at school.

MUM: What?

NICHOLAE: And it's all my fault because her clothes aren't clean and she won't have a bath even though I tell her and sometimes her dress isn't ironed properly because I don't know how to get the creases out and that iron gets too hot and leaves brown marks on the clothes. But it's not my fault. It's your fault. I'm not her parent. You are. You're the parent. I'm just the kid. I'm just the kid!

He cries.

MUM goes to hold him.

MUM: I'm sorry, Nicholae. I'm sorry.

NICHOLAE: Leave me alone. We probably would be better off without you. At least if the council was looking after us we wouldn't have to do our own ironing and cooking.

AISHA: Nicholae! I hate you.

ADA and ROBERT enter.

ADA: How sweet! A family reunion.

Roar.

ROBERT: It's alright, Father, we've found them.

ADA: So we're all together at last.

MUM: Leave them. I'll stay but let them go.

ROBERT: She's got her will back.

ADA: That's soon remedied.

ROBERT: Mother!

Hissing sound.

ADA: My great niece is quite resourceful. I think she takes after me. Don't you think she takes after me? But it's the boy that has the Gift, isn't it? And of course he's weak just like your father.

AISHA: No, he's not.

MUM: Let them go, please.

ADA: Oh she's so frightened. Come Mephista!

Hissing.

AISHA: Leave her alone, you horrible old witch.

ADA: Robert! Silence her!

ROBERT goes to get AISHA.

NICHOLAE steps in his way.

NICHOLAE: Don't touch her.

ROBERT: I shall throw you into the bottomless pit and then I shall eat you.

NICHOLAE: Just try it, fart face!

ROBERT: Ada!

NICHOLAE: Snot nose!

AISHA: (*Prompting NICHOLAE.*) Dogbreath.

NICHOLAE: Dogbreath!

AISHA: Cowardy custard.

NICHOLAE: Cowardy custard.

ROBERT: Ada, they're frightening me.

AISHA: She can't help you. She's scared too. She's scared because she knows that nobody loves her. Her Daddy didn't love her. She thinks the One loves her but he's just using her to get Mum.

ADA: Be quiet!

MUM: There was someone who loved her.

They look at her.

My father loved her. He loved his big sister. He said nobody understood her.

ADA: He was a weakling.

MUM: But he loved you.

ADA: No.

AISHA: And she let Robert kill him. The only person who loved her. And now she's all alone.

ADA: No.

Hissing.

ROBERT: No Mother.

NICHOLAE: Be quiet, you or I'll twist your ear off.

ROBERT: Arrrgh!

ADA: Do something, Robert. She's coming for us.

Hissing increases.

ROBERT: Father! Stop her!

ADA: Daddy! I want my Daddy.

They both scream.

Hissing sound goes.

ADA: Look what you've done. You've ruined us.

ROBERT: I can't believe she'd –

ADA: We'll have to follow her –

ROBERT: Yes.

ADA: We're coming Mephista.

ROBERT: Wait for us, Mother.

AISHA: You don't have to.

NICHOLAE: Aisha!

AISHA: You could come with us. We're going to escape.

ADA: You silly girl! How can we go with you? We have no will. Come, Robert.

She goes.

ROBERT: Kids. I hate 'em.

He runs after ADA.

Roaring sound.

AISHA: It's The One.

MUM: He's angry.

AISHA: Come home with us, Mum.

Roaring sound gets louder.

Is he coming to get us?

MUM: I won't let him. Nicholae?

NICHOLAE: What?

MUM: I'll come home. I promise. But you have to go on without me.

AISHA: No.

MUM: It's the only way, Aisha. I'm linked to him. I must poison him so that he can never cross over the rift.

NICHOLAE: How are you going to do that?

MUM: By thinking happy thoughts. He can't stand happy thoughts. Once he's dead, I'll follow.

AISHA: But what if – ?

MUM: You have to trust me. And you mustn't look back. Not once. If you look back, I'll feel it. I'll know that at that moment you're not trusting me. I need you to trust me if I am to succeed. Will you trust me?

AISHA: Of course.

MUM: Nicholae, do you trust me?

NICHOLAE: Yes.

MUM: You see that door there? It's the back way out. It will lead you to the forest.

AISHA: And you'll come?

MUM: Trust me. Now go on.

Roaring sound gets louder.

Go! And don't look back.

Roaring sound even louder.

AISHA and NICHOLAE go.

MUM smiles and holds out her arms.

Hello, Dietrich. I have such wonderful children.

She laughs a happy laugh.

THE ONE roars in pain.

Scene 16

The Forest. Everything is green. Birds are singing.

NICHOLAE: We're back in the forest.

AISHA: But everything's green and there are birds. We must have been down there for ages.

NICHOLAE: I think the mountain's this way.

AISHA: Do you think – ?

NICHOLAE: What?

AISHA: Do you think she's alright?

NICHOLAE: Don't look back.

AISHA: But what if The One –

NICHOLAE: She said we have to trust her. Come on.

The RAT appears.

RAT: Yippee. We're free. We're all free. All the rooms are emptying and all the Flesheaters are dying and the wills are returning to the bodies from where they were taken. And it's spring! It's spring!

NICHOLAE: It was winter before.

RAT: My mother always used to say that in the heart of winter life is born.

AISHA: Look!

BEHAN enters with a suitcase.

Behan?

GUARDIAN: Yes.

AISHA: I thought so.

GUARDIAN: Found your mother, did you?

NICHOLAE: Yes we did.

AISHA: Aren't you guarding the forest any more?

GUARDIAN: Left my post. Gotta go and meet my brothers. Haven't seen them for years. Big reunion. Very happy. La di da. Toodle pip.

He hurries off.

NICHOLAE turns to watch.

AISHA: Don't look back, Nicholae.

NICHOLAE: I forgot.

They continue.

AISHA: There's still snow on the mountain.

RAT: It's melting though.

NICHOLAE: There are clouds on the top.

RAT: Theodore. Look there's Theodore.

The silver animal enters.

AISHA: That's Theodore?

RAT: Yes.

He runs to THEODORE and there is much squeaking for joy.

NICHOLAE: He doesn't look much like you.

RAT: He comes from the squirrel side of the family.

THEODORE indicates they should follow him like before.

THEODORE:
Follow me through the snow
up the mountainside we go
soon the sky will start to clear
a happy end is very near
one last test and then you're through
your future is awaiting you.
Tears and laughter, joy and strife
all are necessary to life.

AISH/NICH:
Can we make it?
What's the test?
I'm so tired
I want to rest.
Want to see
if Mum is there.
Can't look back
must take care.
Find the gateway
through we go
but can't see it
in the snow.
Snow is blinding
want our mum.
Is our story
nearly done?

AISHA: It's too hard. I want to see if she's following.

NICHOLAE: Don't.

THEODORE indicates they should go on.

RAT: Theo says this is where we part, kids.

THEODORE indicates again.

You go that way.

NICHOLAE: I can feel the Gateway, Aisha. It's very close.

THEODORE squeaks excitedly.

RAT: He says he knew it was here somewhere.

NICHOLAE: Come on.

They stop suddenly. They are on the edge on an abyss.

RAT: What's wrong?

AISHA: It's the edge of a cliff.

RAT: That's right.

AISHA: We'll fall.

THEODORE squeaks.

RAT: He says you have to trust. Hope you make it home.
We're going to go back to the fields and play in the
sunshine. Theo will soon have his summer coat. Bye.

THEODORE and RAT go.

AISHA: It's so high.

They look down.

Do you think Mum's there?

They want to look back.

NICHOLAE: We mustn't.

AISHA: What if she never comes back?

NICHOLAE: She needs us to trust her. Do you trust her?

AISHA nods.

So do I.

They look down.

Come on Aisha.

AISHA: You think we should?

NICHOLAE: We have to.

They hold hands and step out into the abyss.

AISHA: It's cold.

NICHOLAE: It's freezing.

AISHA: I can only see white.

NICHOLAE: We're falling, falling, falling.

They pass a bag of frozen peas. And a packet of fish fingers.
Sound changes.
They step out of the fridge.

AISHA: We made it.

They look round.

She's not here.

NICHOLAE sits down and buries his head in his hands.

I'm starving.

NICHOLAE doesn't answer.

AISHA gets out some biscuits. She offers one to NICHOLAE.

He doesn't respond.

MUM enters in her dressing gown.

MUM: I've lost an earring!

AISHA: Mum.

They rush to her and hug her.

NICHOLAE: You're back.

MUM: Make me a cup of tea, will you?

NICHOLAE picks up the kettle.

AISHA: I'll do it.

He hands her the kettle. He sits with MUM and watches AISHA plug it in.

NICHOLAE: Here's your earring.

MUM: Thank you. Where did you find it?

NICHOLAE: Lying around.

MUM: (*Putting in the earring.*) Then I'll see what's in the fridge.

NICHOLAE looks at her.

Food.

NICHOLAE: Oh.

MUM: You two fancy Tarka Dal tonight?

They nod.

She smiles at them.

Palace of Fear:
The Story

I THINK THEY'RE CALLED Nicholae and Aisha. Nicholae is 11 and Aisha is 9 and things are a bit sad at home at the moment because Dad's left.

Nicholae and Aisha are sad. And Mum is very sad. She cries a lot and lies in bed all the time. When they come home from school she's in bed and there's no tea on the table so Nicholae and Aisha have to make the tea. Nicholae gets the fish fingers out of the fridge and Aisha gets the peas out of the freezer but Nicholae doesn't let Aisha boil the water because she's only 9 and 9 year olds shouldn't deal with boiling water. They put our three portions of food and Nicholae takes some up to Mum but when he goes back after tea she hasn't touched it.

In the mornings they have to find clean clothes and get dressed on their own. Nicholae irons his shirt and Aisha's blouse because he doesn't think nine year olds should use hot irons.

And nobody else knows about it. They don't tell anyone at school and there's no-one else to tell. They don't want to tell anyone.

One day they come home from school and there's a strange woman standing on the doorstep,

'Hello,' she says, 'You must be Nicholae. Haven't you grown?' Don't they always say that? 'I'm your Aunty Ada. And this must Aisha. Goodness me I haven't see you since you were a tiny little baby'

And she smiled one of those smiles that are really big but disappear as suddenly as they come. And when she smiled her eyes weren't smiling at all.

'Now your Mummy's had to go away and so Uncle Robert and I have come to look after you! Robert!' A man appeared at the kitchen door and came down the hall. He looked at them and said, 'Hi kids!'

And Nicholae thought to himself, 'I don't like you!'

And Aisha thought to herself, 'You're scary!'

'Now,' said Aunty Ada, 'I've made you some tea. Do you like steak?'

She sat them down at the kitchen table and gave them two huge pieces of steak. And when they cut into it, it was all red and blood came out of it and ran all over the plate.

'I'm not eating this,' thought Nicholae.

'That's disgusting,' thought Aisha.

And when Aunty Ada wasn't looking they put it in their pockets. Later when they were getting ready for bed they threw it into the toilet and it turned the water all red.

That night in their bedroom Nicholae whispered to Aisha. 'I didn't know we had an Aunty Ada and Uncle Robert. I don't think they're who they say they are. I want to creep down and maybe we'll catch them out and find out who they really are.'

'I'm coming too!' said Aisha.

Nicholae opened the bedroom door and as he did so he thought he saw something out of the corner of his eye. A long twisty something that moved across the landing. But unfortunately as he opened the door wider to take a better look the door creaked and the long twisty thing disappeared into the skirting board by the toilet. It just wasn't there! And a voice from downstairs said, 'Children! I hope you trying to get to sleep!'

Nicholae closed the bedroom door and said, 'Well try again tomorrow! They're cleverer than I thought. I think they're watching and so as soon as they know we're coming they change back.'

'Change back?' asked Aisha.

'From what they really are into Robert and Ada,' said Nicholae.

The next day on the way back from school they stopped off at the bicycle shop and bought one of those little cans of oil with a pointed plastic top that you use for oiling your bike. Nicholae slipped it into his pocket just as they got home where Aunty Ada was waiting on the doorstep,

'Hello, children,' she said flashing them one of her false smiles, 'Your tea's ready! I hope you like sushi!'

Now Nicholae and Aisha didn't know what sushi was. Let me tell you. It's RAW FISH!!! I bet you think Ugghhh. That's exactly what both Nicholae and Aisha thought! And again when Aunty Ada wasn't looking they hid it in their pockets and flushed it down the toilet as before.

In the bedroom Nicholae said, 'Right we're going to catch them tonight.

'Where do you think they're from?' asked Aisha.

'From another world, of course,' said Nicholae confidently as he oiled the hinge on the bedroom door with the oil from the bike shop. 'And they don't want us to know but if we could just get downstairs without them hearing us then we'd find out what they really are.'

'Do you think they're from somewhere where I could be a princess?' asked Aisha.

'No,' said Nicholae and he rolled his eyes because Aisha always wanted to be a princess, 'No,' he repeated, 'Somewhere where I can be a soldier!'

And Aisha rolled her eyes because Nicholae always wanted to be a soldier.

Nicholae opened the door and this time it did not creak. The crept out onto the landing and started to go downstairs. They could see the kitchen door and could hear strange noises coming from the kitchen - a sort of moany groany burpy sort of sound.

You'd have thought, wouldn't you, that Nicholae and Aisha would have gone no further? But what do you think they did? Yes, that's right they went on down. But just as they put their feet on the bottom stair the floorboard made the most horrendous crack and immediately the noise stopped and the door flew open and there was Aunty Ada smiling her falsest of false smiles.

'What do you want?' she asked.

'Uhhhh, uhhhh..........we're thirsty. Can we have a drink of water?'

Have you ever done that? It's always a good way of getting some time out of bed isn't it?

'Here you are,' said Aunty Ada handing them each a glass of water as she sent them back upstairs.

In the bedroom Nicholae said, 'We'll have to try again tomorrow.'

But tomorrow was Saturday and there was no school. When they got up Aunty Ada said, 'Come on, we're going to go and see your Mummy'

'Aha,' thought Nicholae.

'Oh good,' thought Aisha.

When they went outside they saw Uncle Robert's car. It was completely black. Even the windows were black. You couldn't see in at all.

'Nobody will be able to see us when we're in there,' whispered Nicholae.

'Where are they going to take us?' whispered Aisha.

'Come on, kids, get in,' said Uncle Robert and he reached out to open the door. As he did so the sleeve of his jacket rode up his arm and Nicholae could see a tattoo on his arm. A tattoo of a SKULL!!!!!!!! And underneath were the letters D - E - A - T - H. Yes, that's right it said DEATH. And when Uncle Robert saw Nicholae looking he quickly pulled down his sleeve and opened the door.

It was strange because from inside you could see out even though you couldn't see in. 'Now we're for it,' thought Nicholae.

'Maybe they're going to take us to their land,' thought Aisha.

But they drove along the road towards the hospital and parked in the car park. They went into the building and took the lift to the second floor. They walked along a corridor that had lino that made their trainers squeak, to a room at the end. There in a corner was a bed. And in the bed was Mum.

Nicholae ran up to her and said, 'Mum!'
But Mum turned to him and her eyes looked through him. She waved her hand in front of her face and shook her head as if she was very confused.
'Mum, it's us,' said Aisha. And Mum shook her head again and closed her eyes. IT WAS AS IF SHE DIDN'T EVEN RECOGNISE THEM.

At the door a nurse was talking to Aunty Ada and Nicholae heard her say, 'She's not herself..........................'
That explained everything. Nicholae knew immediately what it meant. This was not Mum. Aunty Ada and Uncle Robert had stolen Mum and put a zombie in her place.

He explained it all that night to Aisha. 'That's why we have to get downstairs and find out what they are and where they're from,' he told her. 'Come on! But remember, we have to catch them out!'
Once again they opened the door and crept along the landing. They started to go downstairs and once again they could hear the moany groany burpy sound coming from the kitchen. And from under the kitchen door there came a light brighter than any light they'd seen coming from there. And there was something like smoke or steam seeping out from under the door drifting in the beam.

They reached the last step and remembered not to tread on it. They stepped over it and moved towards the kitchen door.
Nicholae hesitated. Suddenly he wasn't so sure.

It was Aisha that reached out her hand and opened the door. The light was blinding. It was so bright that they could hardly see the kitchen at all. They couldn't see the table or chairs, they couldn't see the sink, they couldn't see the back door with Dad's coat hanging on it - the one he left behind when he went. All they could see was light. And it was coming from the fridge. They moved closer to it squinting to stop the light hurting their eyes. They looked into the fridge but they couldn't see anything. Not the dried up carrot at the back, not the can of beans that had gone mouldy, not the cans of beer that Uncle Robert had put in there. Nothing.

'I know what this is,' said Nicholae, 'This is a PORTAL.'

Now Aisha didn't know what a portal was so Nicholae explained that it led into another dimension. And Aisha saw pictures of princesses in pink dresses in her head.

'We have to go through,' he said, and wondered whether maybe there were soldiers on the other side.

So they stepped into the fridge. Into the light. Into the cold.

And suddenly they were standing on top of a mountain, in the snow, in their pyjamas. Without even any slippers on their feet!

Up above was blue sky and big birds flying. And there just ahead of them in the snow was a little silver furry animal standing on his hind legs and looking at them. Suddenly he jerked his head as if to say, follow me.

'He wants us to follow him,' said Aisha.

So they followed him though the snow leaving footprints behind them. Down the mountain they went, down and down and down. Suddenly they saw something in the ground. Something frozen into the ice. They looked and saw that it was some keys. And the key ring was in the shape of a dog's paw. It was the key ring that Nicholae had bought Mum for Christmas to remind her of their dog, Rex who died.

'It's Mum's keys,' said Aisha.

'She must have come this way,' said Nicholae.

The followed the furry animal down further until the snow thinned out and they began to see plants coming through and they realised they were on a path. The little silver furry animal looked at them as if to say, 'Follow this path,' So they followed the path.

Though fields and beside a stream and over a stile until they came to a forest. And there ahead of them beside the path at the entrance to the forest was a fallen tree trunk. And on the fallen tree trunk there was the strangest figure they had ever seen. He had strange wires coming out of his head and was making a loud snoring noise.

'Hello' said Nicholae.
But he didn't wake up.
'Hey you!' said Aisha.
But still he slept.
'Hey,' said Nicholae touching one of the creature's wires.
'What? What? What?' he said jumping up and looking around in all directions. Then he saw the children. 'Who are you? What do you want?'
'Have you seen our Mum?' asked Aisha.
'What's a Mum?' said the creature.
'A Mother,' Nicholae replied.
'Never heard of them,' said the creature.
'It's a person who helps you to grow up,' said Aisha, 'A big person, a grown up.'
'Bigger than you?' he asked.
'Yes,' said Aisha.
'No people big or small have come past here in days. I am the guardian of the forest and I haven't seen anyone.
'But you were asleep,' said Nicholae.
'I was not,' said the creature, 'I never sleep.'
'Is our Mum in the forest?' asked Aisha.
'How should I know?' said the creature. 'But you should know that no-one who goes into that forest ever comes out again. There's a WHATEVERITIS in there that will steal your

mind. You have to keep very still if you hear the birds start to sing warnings or if the leaves start to rustle loudly in the wind. And above all you mustn't talk when the WHATEVERITIS is around because it uses your words to climb through your mouth and into your mind. And it will steal your mind and you will never find it again.'

And having said this the creature with the wires coming out of his head fell fast asleep again.

Now you'd have thought, wouldn't you, that after hearing this, the last thing that Nicholae and Aisha would have done is to have gone into the forest. And what do you think they did. Yes, that's right! They went into the forest.

They walked under the trees and through the leaves until it started to get dark. Suddenly they heard the birds begin to whistle warnings and leaves rustled in the trees like they were whispering of danger approaching.

'Sleeping Lions!' said Nicholae.

Sleeping Lions was a game they had played at Nicholae's last birthday party and Aisha knew that it meant you had to lie on the floor with your eyes closed and stay as still and as quiet as possible.

So that is what they did.

All around them they heard voices, snatches of conversation, like things that might come out of a person's mind if you held it upside down and shook it. Snatches of song and smells and memories.

Nicholae thought he smelt a bacon sandwich and then dog poo and Aisha thought she could smell the smell of Mum just after she had got out of the bath. And she thought she heard her voice singing:

Twinkle, twinkle, chocolate bar,
My Mum drives a rusty car,
Start the engine, pull the choke
Off we go in a cloud of smoke,
Twinkle twinkle chocolate bar

My Mum drives a rusty car.

It was the song Mum used to sing them at night to get them to go to sleep.

The WHATEVERITIS seemed to be moving away. When the leaves and the birds grew quieter Nicholae and Aisha stood up and followed in the direction that they thought it had gone. They could hear the leaves rustle and the birds whistle further in the forest. They followed it under the trees and through the bushes. Sometimes it looked like a slimy thing with three heads and sometimes it looked like a bear. Sometimes it was like a grey ghost and sometimes it looked like a vampire with blood dripping from its mouth. This was the thing about the WHATEVERITIS it changed it's shape depending on what you found most scary.

It was now very dark but the moon shone down through the trees and they saw the WHATEVERITIS stand before a big rock.

It stood there and spoke:

I AM THE THING THAT PEOPLE MOST FEAR
THEY LOSE THEIR MINDS WHEN I AM NEAR
SO I GATHER THEM UP AND BRING THEM DOWN
TO THE ONE WHO WEARS THE DEATHLY CROWN.
I HAVE THOUGHTS AND DREAMS AND MEMORIES TOO
SO OPEN THE ROCK AND LET ME PASS THROUGH.

And the rock made a sort of hissing sound and opened wide and the WHATEVERITIS passed through.

Now everyone always said that Nicholae had a terrible memory when it came to learning things off by heart. But without hesitating he stood in front of the rock and said:

I AM THE THING THAT PEOPLE MOST FEAR
THEY LOSE THEIR MINDS WHEN I AM NEAR
SO I GATHER THEM UP AND BRING THEM DOWN
TO THE ONE WHO WEARS THE DEATHLY CROWN.

*I HAVE THOUGHTS AND DREAMS AND MEMORIES TOO
SO OPEN THE ROCK AND LET ME PASS THROUGH.*

And once again the rock made a hissing noise and the children passed through following the WHATEVERITIS. They were in a dark cave but they could hear it moving ahead of them and so they followed it down into the earth. Down and down and down - sometimes they heard the voices like the ones they had heard in the forest, sometimes they smelt things – once Nicholae was sure he smelt Mum's perfume.

Then they heard nothing. They turned a corner and saw a huge cavern with an Underground lake. And on the lake was a boat. And in the boat was a figure and as soon as they set eyes on this person the children felt better.

'Ah there you are at last,' the person said, 'I've been waiting for you. I'm here to help you.'

Now the WHATEVERITIS could change its shape depending on what you find most scary as I told you. And the person in the boat was the same. It too changed its shape depending on what you found most reassuring. Sometimes it looked like Mum's friend Trudy and sometimes it looked like Mum. Sometimes it looked like Dad and sometimes it looked like a spirit.

'I am going to row you across the lake and show you how to get down to the palace of the One Who Wears The Deathly Crown,' the person told them. 'But you must be very careful because the palace is guarded by three dogs each bigger and more frightening than the last.

The first cannot see you, smell you, or hear you, but it will feel your warmth.

The second dog is in a very dark place and he cannot hear you or smell you but he will see the light that shines from your eyes.

And the third dog is the worst of the lot. He can only do one thing. He will smell your fear.

If you get past the dogs you will find yourself in the palace. Now the palace of The One Who Wears The Deathly Crown has many rooms. Maybe your mother is in one of these rooms. The thing you should know about these rooms is that each one contains a different fear.'

And with that the person in the boat held out a hand and helped them to step into the boat. Then the person rowed them across the lake and pointed to an opening that led further down into the earth.

'That way,' the person said, 'And good luck!'

Now you'd have thought, wouldn't you, that the last thing that Nicholae and Aisha would do, having heard all this, would be to go in search of the palace? But what do you think they did? Yes, that's right, they entered the opening and followed where the cave led them. It was very gloomy in there. At first they heard and saw nothing and then just ahead they could see the shape of a huge beast. Snoring in a way that sounded like snarling.

Nicholae looked around. To one side there was a small pool of water.

'Get in there!' he said to Aisha.

'What?!' she asked.

'We have to cool down. Get in there!'

And they lay down in the icy cold water and stayed there until their teeth chattered and they were frozen almost to the bone.

'Can we get out now?' asked Aisha.

'I think so,' Nicholae replied.

And they stood up and moved towards the huge beast. The could see it's huge paws and it had slobber dripping from it's mouth and its snores were enough to make your knees turn to jelly. But they edged past and he did not wake because he did not sense any warmth.

The cave got narrower and smaller so that they had to crawl on hands and knees. Once again they saw a shape ahead. It was so big that it almost filled the whole space.

'We have to close our eyes,' said Aisha.

So they closed their eyes and edged past the beast. At one point Nicholae felt its hot breath on his neck and he nearly opened his eyes. But he managed to keep them shut and they got past without being detected.

They went further and the cave got narrower and smaller yet so that they had to crawl. But ahead they could see an opening where the cave got bigger again. Nicholae put his head through and got the shock of his life. Lying underneath the opening was the largest dog he had ever seen, taking up the whole space. There was just a narrow gap between him and the wall to get through.

'We're going to have to be very brave,' he whispered to Aisha.

'Let's sing Mum's song,' she said and then maybe we won't be scared - not if we hold hands.

And that is what they did. They crawled through the opening and edged past the dog holding hands and singing,

Twinkle, twinkle, chocolate bar,
My Mum drives a rusty car,
Start the engine, pull the choke
Off we go in a cloud of smoke,
Twinkle twinkle chocolate bar
My Mum drives a rusty car.

The could see the dog's huge jaws that could crush you in the flash on an eye. They could see its sharp teeth all glistening and yellow and they could smell the most horrible smell coming from it's mouth.

'I think I'm getting frightened,' Aisha whispered to Nicholae.

'Keep singing,' said Nicholae squeezing her hand.

And they kept singing and thought of Mum and managed to get past.

Whew!

And they found themselves in a huge cavern with stalagmites soaring up into the air and stalactites hanging down from above - all colours of the rainbow. And in the rocks all round there were doors. Doors leading into the rooms from which came groans and screams and whimpers. And each room held a different fear.

One room was full of spiders. Spiders everywhere that looked like jewels. But when you picked them up you realised they were spiders. ARACHNOPHOBIA it said on the door.

'That means fear of spiders,' said Nicholae.

'I think I've got that,' said Aisha.

One room had a pool with sea creatures that would electrocute you and so that you couldn't move and then the water would rise and drown you. That one had HYDROPHOBIA written on its door. One room contained the fear of death and in the wall were trapped voices of the dead. One room had a bomb that threw cement over you that petrified you and turned you to stone. One room stole the glitter from your eyes and its walls were covered with pretty marbles but when you went closer you saw it was eyes.

'Fear of blindness,' whispered Nicholae.

But Mum wasn't in any of these rooms. Finally they came to the room that had CLAUSTROPHOBIA on the door. In it was a person in a box. He was terrified of suffocating in such a close space.

'Come out,' said Nicholae.

'I can't,' said the one who was scared of suffocation.

'Have you seen our Mum?' they asked him.

'I haven't seen anyone in here,' he replied, 'But if you want to know who's come in lately you should go to the vertigo room because in there is someone who is high up on a ledge and he sees everything that goes on. You have to go up the stairs at the end of the corridor.

So they found the stairs and climbed them. Up and up and up. They came to a small room with a window. But there was no-one in there. They looked out and saw that there was someone standing on a ledge on the wall. Nicholae and Aisha looked out and realised just how high they were. There was a sheer drop.

'Hello,' said Nicholae to the man on the ledge but he didn't hear him.

'Hello,' said Aisha.

But he was too far away, clinging to the wall and unable to move.

'We're going to have to climb out to him,' Aisha told her brother.

And she climbed out on the ledge.

Nicholae hesitated.

'Come on,' Aisha said to him.

And looking very pale Nicholae climbed out of the window onto the narrow ledge.

'Don't look down,' Aisha said.

But it was too late, Nicholae had already done so and he felt a sort of fluttery jittery feeling in his stomach like the feeling he used to get when Dad drove the car over the hump back bridge when they used to go and visit their Gran in the country. It really was the most unpleasant feeling. Nicholae's legs turned to jelly and he just wanted to cling to the wall and not move at all – like the man further along the ledge.

Aisha gave him her hand.

'Just move an inch at a time,' she told him.

And slowly they moved forward. Inch by inch by inch until they were standing beside the frozen man.

'Please Sir,' said Aisha.

'Go away!' said the man hardly moving his lips so scared was he of any movement.

'But we want to know if you've seen our Mum,' she explained to him. 'She's got brown hair and wears bright clothes.'

'Smells of bath soap and sings a song about rusty cars?' asked the man who almost forgot to be frightened for a moment.

'That's her,' said Aisha.

'She's the one whose fear is loneliness. She's scared of being on her own,' said the man. 'No-one knows where the One Who Wears The Deathly Crown has put her but it's somewhere far away from anyone else in a secret place that only the One knows.'

'We have to find her,' Aisha explained.

'Then you'll have to go and ask The One Who Wears The Deathly Crown,' he said, 'His throne room is that way!'

And barely moving his head he indicated along the ledge to an opening in the wall where there were stairs leading up further.

'We'll have to get past you,' said Aisha.

'Be careful, won't you?' he asked fearfully.

'Tell me something,' said Aisha.

'What?' said the man.

'If you're so scared of heights, why do you stay here? You could just climb back in the window. Everyone here is so silly. They're scared of spiders but the live in a room full of spiders. Or they're scared of water and they live in a pool.'

'Don't you understand anything?' said the man. 'That's the point. You always hold on to the thing you fear. You hold it close to you and refuse to give it up. It's like you wouldn't exist without it.'

'Well I think that's a load of rubbish,' said Aisha and she started to edge along the ledge past the one who was scared of heights.

'I can't,' said Nicholae, 'I want to stay here.'

'Don't be silly,' you can't stay here said Aisha.

'I want to,' said Nicholae.

'Please Nicholae,' said Aisha, 'Mum needs us. She's all alone.'

And Nicholae thought of Mum all alone in a place where there was no-one else and suddenly he felt something that he had never felt before. It was like he was the parent and she was the child and he imagined her all sad and lonely and needing someone to give her a kiss. It was a warm feeling but it felt painful at the same time.

And the feeling was so strong that it made him brave and he took a step along the ledge and edged past the one who was scared of heights.

'You don't have to stay here, you could move,' he whispered to him as he passed. But the one who was scared of height was too petrified to listen.

And so Nicholae joined Aisha at the end of the ledge and crawled in to the opening with the stairs that led up to a big doorway.

It was the doorway to the throne-room of The One Who Wears The Deathly Crown.

Many are the legends that have grown up about what happened in the throne room of the One Who Wears The Deathly Crown. Nicholae and Aisha never talked about it – maybe because it was so frightening. Some say that they had to get the deathly crown and in the process Nicholae was turned to stone and Aisha had to complete tasks to save him, others say that they both had to complete three tasks – to get keys by going through deathly fire, to open doors guarded by a knife thrower, to get beneath a quaking bridge, there are rumours of challenges involving dogs with five heads and challenges where they had to scrub the floor of the throne room. In one report it is said that they had to race the One With The Deathly Crown himself and that Aisha tricked him by tying his legs together. There is a one story, that recounts how they were helped by the One's servant. It is said that she took the poison out of the three frogs that the One told them to eat. When they pretended to be dead from eating the frogs they heard the One talk about where their Mum was imprisoned. In some versions of the legend it is said that they saw the tattoo on the One's arm – the same tattoo that Uncle Robert had, some even say that The One was Uncle Robert and that he resided in a room of fear where the God and Goddess of fear fed him evil. Others say that the One was Blind and that he sent Aisha and Nicholae to find him eyes. Or that he had a powerful sceptre and in yet another Aisha found a necklace that gave her more power. There are tales of two bodyguards one was half bee and half human, the other half lion and half human. In yet another version of the legend the One had two servants who were children who were also looking for their mother – the little girl stood by the One's throne stroking her pet rabbit. In this legend Aisha and Nicholae killed the One.

The one thing on which all versions of the legend agree is that Aisha and Nicholae defeated the One and they left the throne room knowing exactly where Mum was to be found.

They had to walk along a long corridor that seemed as if it stretched forever into the distance. Above them cameras moved and followed their progress and on each side of them were filing cabinets. The first one had a label which said A-AA. Nicholae opened it and found a file where he read: A Aaron, Fear: Agoraphobia Location: The room of open spaces, Another said B Aarka, Fear: Xenophobia, Location: The Room of Many Races and Nations.

'Come on, Nicholae,' urged Aisha, 'We have to find Mum.'

And they walked along the long endless corridor under flickering light bulbs. At the filing cabinet marked M they found Mum's file Fear: Loneliness, Location: The Room of Isolation.

So they walked and walked and the way got dustier and dirtier. They saw the skeleton of a mouse that had ventured this far and had obviously expired for lack of food. There were bones and cobwebs hanging down from the ceiling. It seemed that no-one had been this way for years.

'Do you really think she's here?' asked Aisha.

'This is the way that the One told us,' Nicholae replied.

And it was so quiet down there, so deathly quiet. It was a quiet that made you feel you were the last person alive in the whole world. Eventually after many hours they came to a door obscured by cobwebs which they tore at and removed.

On the door was written in red NO ENTRY.

Now you'd have thought, wouldn't you, that when they read that, Nicholae and Aisha would have gone no further? But what do you think they did? That's right, they decided to open the door. But it was locked.

'We'll have to pick the lock,' said Aisha.

'What with?' Nicholae asked her.

'Let's look in our pockets,' she said.

But they had nothing. All that Nicholae found was............Mum's keys.

'Try them,' Aisha told him.

'They won't fit,' he said.

'How do you know unless you try?' she answered.

One of the keys, the Yale key for their own front door, looked like it might fit. Nicholae inserted it in the lock and turned.........and pushed.........and the door opened.

Nicholae found themselves in an empty room. Empty except for a bed. And in the bed was a woman. It was Mum.

Nicholae and Aisha rushed towards her but as soon as she saw them tears brimmed up in Mum's eyes and ran down her cheeks,

'No, no, no,' she said, 'You mustn't come in here. You must go'

'But we've come to rescue you,' Nicholae told her.

'We've come to take you home,' said Aisha.

'No, I can't come home,' Mum said shaking her head and crying more, 'If I go home I will be lonely.'

'But if you stay here you'll be lonely too,' said Nicholae.

'But here I'm safe, I know what to expect,' she said, 'At home I might I forget to be lonely for a while but then something will happen and I'll be lonely again and I'd rather stay here. Here I know how things are.'

'You won't be lonely,' said Nicholae, 'We'll be there.'

'You don't need me. You'd be better off without me, I'm bad,' she told them, 'Your father left and everything I do is bad. I'm a bad mother. I'm no use to you.'

'But we need you. You have to make our food like only you can do,' Nicholae said.

'And only you know how to brush my hair so that it doesn't hurt,' said Aisha.

'And only you know how to rub my knee when I come off my bike,' said Nicholae.

'And only you know how to make me feel better when I've got a fever,' said Aisha.

'And only you know how to make the bad dreams go away in the night,' said Nicholae.

'And besides,' said Aisha, 'Next week is your birthday and I've got you a surprise. Don't you want to know what it is?'

'Maybe,' said Mum.

'If you don't come back,' said Nicholae, 'We won't grow up. We need you to help us to become adults.'

'We love you Mum,' Aisha told her.

And Mum started to cry again. And Aisha stroked her hand. And Nicholae stroked her arm. And it reminded him of what Mum used to do when he woke up in the night.

And Nicholae started to sing:
Twinkle, twinkle, chocolate bar,
My Mum drives a rusty car,

And Aisha joined in.

Start the engine, pull the choke
Off we go in a cloud of smoke,
Twinkle twinkle chocolate bar
My Mum drives a rusty car.

And Mum looked at them as if she was seeing them for the first time.

'You think I should really come back?' she asked.

'Of course,' they chorused.

'Here,' said Nicholae, 'here are your keys. You won't be able to get in the house without them.'

'Do you have enough faith?' she asked them pulling them to her.

'Faith?' Aisha asked her.

'Faith and trust that if I say I will come home you will believe me.'

'Of course we believe you,' Nicholae said.

'Then you must go through that door,' she said pointing to some velvet curtains, 'You must leave through that door and you must never look back. You must trust that I will follow. If you look back then I will have to stay here forever. Can you do that?' And she looked into their eyes as if her life depended on it.

'I think so,' said Aisha.

'Then go,' said Mum, 'And trust!'

And she pushed them towards the door.

'But – ' said Nicholae.

'What if – ?' said Aisha.

'Don't look back,' Mum ordered.

And they pulled back the velvet curtains and there was a fire door with two bars. And on the door were written the words. NO EXIT. Nicholae put his hands on one bar and Aisha put her hands on the other bar and they pushed. The doors flew open and they saw trees and leaves and heard birds. They had come out the back way. They had missed out the long corridor and the throne room and the palace with all its rooms. They had missed out the cave with the three dogs and the lake with the boat. They had missed out the sliding door in the rock. They were back in the forest.

Nicholae wanted to look back into the room of isolation to see if Mum was following but Aisha said,

'Come on, don't look back.'

So they walked through the forest with leaves falling all around them. When they last passed through all the leaves had been green like in the spring but while they had been in the palace of The One the season had changed and now it was autumn.

They walked through the forest safely without seeing any sign of the WHATEVERITIS until they came to the very edge where there was a fallen tree trunk. Sitting on the trunk was the strange creature with wires coming out of his head. It was the guardian of the forest. Fast asleep as usual. This time they did not wake him. They wanted to take one last look into the forest to see if Mum was behind them but they managed to resist the temptation. They passed along the path over the stile and beside a stream and through fields until it started to climb. The air got colder and they started to see snow on the ground. It lay thicker than before because winter was coming. So they walked through the snow. In their pyjamas. Without even slippers on their feet. Everything looked different as they climbed the mountain.

'How will we find the portal?' asked Aisha.

'I don't know,' Nicholae replied.

They came to the top of the mountain and looked around. They could see no sign of any funny gap in the world through which they could pass.

'Look,' said Aisha suddenly.

There in the snow was a little furry creature. They recognised him even though his silver coat had turned white.

He stood on his hind legs and looked at them. Suddenly he jerked his head.

'He wants us to follow,' Aisha said like before.

The furry creature led them to edge of the mountain. If you looked down you could see an abyss of white ice and snow. Nicholae's stomach turned as he looked down.

The little furry creature jerked his head once more.

'We have to go over the edge,' said Aisha.

'We can't,' said Nicholae nervously.

They were so high and there was so far to fall.

'But we have to, Nicholae. Mum needs us.'

More than ever, Nicholae wanted to look back, to see if Mum was following. What was the point of all this if she didn't even come back?

'Don't look back!' said Aisha.

And he thought about Mum and it gave him the same painful feeling in his stomach that he had felt on the ledge.

So he took Aisha's hand and said,

'I really love Mum.'

And Aisha said, 'So do I.'

And then

        they stepped

              out

                    into

                        the

                            a

                              i

                              r

And they were falling. And it was cold. Icy cold. And all they could see was white. White, white, white! And so cold, cold, cold.

And then they saw something, floating towards them. It was green and there was writing on it. It was a packet of frozen peas. And then they saw something else. It was a dried up carrot that had curled up and gone brown at the end. And suddenly they were stepping out of the fridge. And there, standing before them, was Mum.

And she said,

'There you are! I've been worried out of my mind!'

And she took them in her arms and hugged them to her. And she smelt of soap and shampoo. It was the smell she always had when she had just stepped out of the bath. It was a beautiful smell.

'I don't know why you're looking in the fridge. I've put your dinner on the table,' she told them.

And there on the table was their favourite dinner.
Mum pointed to their chairs.
'Eat up!' she said.

The End